CHOOSE TO BE HAPPY

RUDRA PRESS ✾ PORTLAND, OREGON

CHOOSE TO BE HAPPY

The Craft

and the Art of

Living Beyond Anxiety

Swami Chetanananda

Rudra Press
PO Box 13390
Portland, Oregon 97213
Telephone: 503-235-0175
Telefax: 503-235-0909

Book and cover design by Bill Stanton
Cover photo courtesy of Seattle Art Museum, *Kama, God of Love*

Chetanananda, Swami
        Choose to be Happy : the craft and the art of living
beyond anxiety / by Swami Chetanananda.
                        p.   cm.
        ISBN 0-915801-48-5 (alk. paper)
        1. Spiritual life. 2. Peace of mind—Religious aspects.
3. Conduct of life. 4. Success—Religious aspects. I. Title.
BL624.C4523 1996
294.5'44—dc20   96-28213
                                                    CIP

Contents

Acknowledgments

I WANT TO THANK several people for their fine work on this book: Bill Stanton for the cover and book design; readers Karen Kreiger, Ellen Hynson, Sharon Ward, Cheryl Rosen, Sean Miller, Joan Ames; and editor Pat Tarzian.

THE PENDULUM

OF LIFE

*T*HE BUDDHA QUANTIFIED the dilemma: People are the source of their own suffering. Our minds tell us, "You need this, you need that. This and that are the meaning of life." And so we grasp for this and that, only to discover that this and that are out-of-reach, do not satisfy or, if they satisfy somewhat, definitely end, as does everything, in sickness, old age and death.

So we say, "What's this? I can't win no matter how I play this game." And that is, unfortunately, rule number one of the Game of Life: You play, you lose—because if your mind doesn't make you unhappy with the state of things, then decay certainly will. It's like this—the one who dies with the most toys loses anyway.

"But if we are alive," we ask, "don't we *have* to play the Game of Life? Isn't playing the game, by definition, living?" The answer, thankfully, is, "No." As long as we don't identify with our individual life, with this body, this mind, in other words, this temporary and implicitly defective arrangement, we are not playing the game; and then winning and losing become irrelevant to us, and "living" takes on a whole different meaning.

Fortunately, there is something more to us than the worldly cycle of quick emergence in birth, rapid flowering in adolescence, and slow decline for the rest of our days. We are each connected to and exist from something that isn't affected by the various cycles of expression and reabsorption intrinsic to our bodily and worldly existence. We are each connected to something that is truly alive—that is really "living"—that has always been alive, will always be alive, no matter who or what passes from this earth. We have to work somewhat consistently to lock into this connection with that which is truly alive in us, but the connection is available to all of us, regardless of our religious, genetic, ethnic, or philosophical backgrounds. And while the work to make this connection is serious, it isn't dreary or beyond any of us.

We all live on this pendulum. It's unavoidable. It simply is what life in the world, surrounded by other people and immersed in our desires, is. We live on a pendulum in which success and failure, happiness and sadness, are constantly rising and falling. We cling to the pendulum because it is what life is, and as the pendulum swings along, we reach out for what we want, or what we think we want.

But intrinsic to the movement of a pendulum is that, invariably, at some point, it moves away from the thing for which we're reaching and towards something else. Back and forth, back and forth. We think, "Okay, I can live with this. I didn't get Door Number Two, but Door Number Three seems to be within my grasp. I want that." We reach out, and again the pendulum moves away from the new desire and back towards the old something else or towards yet another something else. Back and forth, back and forth. Eventually, we become cynical about our prospects. We think we see other people being happy, able to hold on to some juicy tidbit that eludes us. So we say, "Life is nice to the other guy and unfair to me."

But life isn't particularly nice to anyone. Life doesn't do nice things to living beings. This is ironic, but it's also one of the main rules of the Game of Life. It's the corollary to, You play, you lose.

Compare what I'm saying to your own actual experience, not your illusions and fantasies. When you've taken the time to talk to those people you envy, really talk to them about their lives, what do you find? Disease, death, decay. Just like the Buddha said. Some happiness, but always disease, death, decay. They've lost a child, a spouse, a beloved friend. They may look healthy and beautiful to you, but they've got some kind of pain—some disease that maybe won't kill them but will make their lives a little more miserable each year—or whatever. Just like the Buddha said. Because that's life.

So things are hopeless, right? We're just trapped inside some cosmic joke that holds out promises of happiness like sweets on a string and then snatches them away from us. Wrong. Think of that pendulum again. Study it. What do you see? The bottom part of the rod makes a big arc, as does most of the rod itself; the bottom part of the rod and the rod itself have the potential to swing all around. But when you look at the pendulum as a whole, you will notice something very interesting about the top of the rod at the point just above the hinge. That point is perfectly still. The dictionary defines a pendulum as "a body hung from a fixed point so as to swing freely to and fro..." So there is a point on every pendulum which, by definition, does not swing around. Whatever vagaries of fortune haunt the rest of the rod, that stillpoint, that fulcrum point, does not share in them.

And that is the place on which we want to focus. It is the place on the pendulum we want to live from because it puts us above the arm, above the swinging around, above the grasping for this and that. It is the place where, no matter what life is doing to us, we are fine. That point on the pendulum at the top of the arm is completely calm and still, but it is not lifeless; it is in fact the key to our connection to the vitality we spoke of earlier—to that which is truly alive in each of us.

Let me take a moment to explain at the outset that when we discuss stillness in this book, we mean something that is dynamic, a combination of motion and quiet, a peace that is pregnant with a vibrancy. We will look at this combination of vitality and stillness in more detail in Chapter Eight; but for now it's enough to understand that the stillpoint is the place on life's pendulum where we can get a lot or a little, and no matter what, we are happy.

To live from that still place takes work, but once you begin to do that work and to view the pendulum less personally—to see it for what it truly is—you can live on it at the fulcrum, with the bottom of the pendulum moving around like crazy, and not be affected. You're still on the pendulum, but you're living from a different place. Then your experience of the pendulum differs profoundly from someone who lives down on the arm.

To make the whole thing even trickier, life is not just a two-dimensional pendulum, a stick and a weight. It's a string and a weight; it swings all over the place. But we simply have to remember that, stick or string, a pendulum always has a stillpoint. And accessing that stillpoint in order to live from it is where we want to be.

So some of you might be asking, "Just what exactly is this stillpoint? Talking about a pendulum is fine, but where in our *actual* lives do we find the stillpoint, and how do we get to it?" The answer to these questions is simple, but it requires a bit of background.

Let's take an example from childhood. Do you remember when you were a kid on a swing, and you tried to touch something out in front of you? You would swing harder and harder and still never reach that something because while the arcing motion of the swing would give you a sense of forward movement, it would also invariably pull you back. You always went up and fell back, never quite touching your goal. That was the strange thing about swinging—try hard and miss anyway. Just like living on the lower part of the pendulum. Try hard and miss anyway.

The more we struggle to get what we want, the more distance we put between ourselves and the thing we want. Pursuing things is useless; chasing after most things doesn't work. This is the nature of the desires powering the pendulum of life, and that's because we have so little control over so many of the things over which we'd like to think we have control.

When we take an honest look at what we have control over, do we really have—does any of us really have—the control over life necessary to get most of the things we want? Let's look at some of the possibilities. Okay, so we want the Super Value Special at our local supermarket, and we know they're running it today. Fine, we may get a goal like that—if we don't run out of gas on the way to the market or if they don't run out of the special before we get there. Right? Even the simplest, ostensibly most certain things have a way of doubling back and biting us.

But what about some of the more serious things we might want? How many of us have, as our fondest wish, that a loved one who is ill won't die? Look at that wish.

It's natural, it's admirable, but realistic? It's completely out of our hands. We have no control over that, no control whatsoever over death. Whether we believe in some higher form of energy or not, whether we believe in God or whatever or not, we know we can't control death. We know that something else, something many people think of as mysterious and seemingly haphazard, has control over who and what dies, when and how.

So what makes us think we can control life? Death is part of life's continuum. If we have no control over the end product, how can we think we have much control over the assembly line that produces it?

Let's take another example of a common wish—finding a mate. Many people think there's someone for everyone, and that this and that can be done to attract a loving, sharing partner. So the wish for a mate should be possible, we reassure ourselves. Well, if the divorce statistics don't convince us of the error of that thinking, this should: Finding a mate involves the consent, attraction, desires, etcetera of another human being, and the one thing we should all know by now is the futility of controlling, for very long at least, anyone or anything outside ourselves. People have a way of wanting to live their own lives, hold their own opinions, perform their own, independent actions. We may find a mate, we may lose a mate. In other words, we may have some control over ourselves, but we have no control over anyone else.

The fact is that we have no control over ninety—make that ninety-eight—percent of what is going to happen to us. Control is the greatest illusion of all. Granted, we know that if we make no effort on an important exam, nine chances out of ten, we'll flunk; whereas we also know that if we study hard, we probably will pass, even pass well, and eventually become whatever it is we want to be. Effort is definitely necessary. Practice, study, hard work are totally admirable. We certainly can exercise that much control over our lives; we can choose to prevail over our natural desire to be lazy. The fact that the reality of life is that we have no deep control over the outcome of things does not mean that we stop trying to do commendable work.

But it does mean—it absolutely does mean—that we adopt a completely different attitude about what effort is and what we think it's going to get us. Grasping for things gets us nowhere because we have no control over any of it anyway.

Practice letting go, deeply letting go of your desires. Digest—do not become depressed—digest the fact that you have little, if any, control over most things, and then practice letting go of this thing and that thing that you are so certain you cannot live without. Think of something you want very much, and then imagine you will never have it. Swing toward it. There it is. Let go of it. There it goes.

Isn't there an extraordinary feeling of relief, of peace, when you close your eyes, take a deep breath, picture the thing you want to have happen, and then, in another deep breath, let go of it altogether? Isn't there the realization that, no matter what it is, even that deep wish for a loved one's well-being, you can let go of it and leave it to something higher and finer, knowing full well that all of it, even your most trivial desire, is in the control of something higher and finer anyway?

This letting go does not mean that we don't love or care for people. It doesn't mean that we're numb and have no feelings for people. But it does mean that, in order to be happy, we don't need life to give us what we think we want. We can accept that we may never make as much money as we'd like, that the quality of companionship we think we deserve may never happen, and so on. We can live with or without these things and be fine.

> *Happiness is not an external condition into which we stumble; our not getting what we want doesn't mean we can't be happy. It doesn't mean we shouldn't be happy. It does mean that we must take total responsibility for our happiness and not think that some external condition, place, event or person will suddenly make our lives wonderful. We make our lives wonderful. Period.*

If we want to be happy, we have to choose to be happy. If we want wonderful, we have to make it that way. We have to open our hearts every single day and be caring people. Then it doesn't matter how much money we have or that our friends are never perfect; our inner work has begun.

So to answer the question at the beginning of this section: "Where is the stillpoint in our daily lives, and how do we get to it?"—the answer is simple. The stillpoint at the top of the pendulum is not something outside ourselves; the stillpoint is in us. Happiness—that which is truly alive, the stillpoint—is in us. And deep inner work is how we are going to learn to live from that stillpoint and be happy.

In using the pendulum to talk about the up-and-down cycle of public opinion, people sometimes remark that a pendulum has to pass through negative territory in order to gather momentum for its move toward the positive. They use this example to make the observation that if we just wait, everything will go from down to up. This is often true, and something that's useful to remember.

But let's also look at the words, "positive" and "negative," in the analogy. In scientific terms, pendulums may indeed need to pass through negative territory to get to the positive; and in human terms, it may also be true that from difficult periods, we can gather tremendous strength, which can propel us into more productive circumstances. But many people make the observation about negative and positive territory in the swing of the pendulum because they believe that "down" is always negative and "up" is always positive.

But when I look at the pendulum from a different perspective—in the spirit of simple observation—I see an arm moving from right to left and left to right. I do see that part of the arc goes up and that part of it goes down; but it really is up to me if I want to say that one direction is more negative than the other. This is significant because what we perceive as positive or negative in our lives may not be positive or negative at all; and this is important for us to understand because while it is true that if we just wait, everything will go from down to up, it is also true, as long as we're on a moving pendulum, that everything will inevitably go from up to down.

Life is in fact totally integrated on every level; but many of us have trouble seeing this. Most of us are used to thinking of certain things as negative and others as positive, certain things as evil and others as good: Something we do is a bad act, something else is a good one; the devil is the author of bad things, God is good; we need to be good people, we can't be bad. This means that we're in constant conflict with ourselves and with the forces that are greater than ourselves. We are forever asking anxious questions like, "Why do bad things happen to good people?" and "What's going to happen to me?"

But what if this is not a dualistic universe? What if there is no such thing as a devil and only one thing that is God or Vital Force or whatever you choose to call it? What if this higher, finer vibration is the author of everything, and it is only our limited perception that creates the illusion of bad and good—in effect, the illusion that there is anything but one thing and that it all just is what it is?

We wouldn't want to use this non-dualistic view as an excuse to hurt people or to do unproductive things with our lives. But for a moment, let's do use it to see the illusion of bad and good as the self-serving thing that it might be. What we call "bad" is often something that brings us pain, and what we call "good," ease. Yet we all know many activities which are pleasurable or easy that do not promote our highest best interest, and we also know that even the most painful experiences—*especially the most painful*—such as loss of a loved one, or even cruel and abusive behavior, when faced, digested, and surmounted, can turn out to be some of the most maturing and productive events in our lives. Now where's the good here and the bad?

Good and bad are terms which only belong in the psyche of an individual who still believes he or she is in control. Good and bad become irrelevant the minute we acknowledge that something higher than ourselves is running the show and that only that higher element understands why things happen the way they do. Every event simply is what it is: something that higher and finer vibration has caused to happen for whatever reason.

It is obvious to me that everything—what we call good and what we label as bad—has been created by that higher force for our growth—not our ease or our pleasure, but our growth. And this means that everything, including the things we've thought of as bad, are on the side of our growth and can be processed to make us bigger and finer people. Again, where's the good and bad here? It's all good—I didn't say painless, I said "good." Only our limited perception—our attachment to these bodies and minds that measure everything by how gratifying it feels at the time—keeps us from seeing that every moment is a joyous one, every event, a potential gift from that higher understanding.

So now it's time to ask: How do you want to travel in life? Do you want to travel confused or do you want to travel clear? Do you want to travel miserable or happy? It's simple. You do have control over one thing—your attitude—and given that life is a pendulum and that, to a great degree, you have no choice over the rhythms, cycles, and pulse of your material and biological existence, doesn't it seem like a fine idea—perhaps the only idea—first and foremost to set your priorities on what you really can affect? Your understanding. Your attitude. Your joy.

If you want to be happy and live beyond anxiety, it is necessary to see the reality of life and to support that reality in a very simple way, which does not involve striving for and struggling after desires at all. Rather than focusing on desires and the illusion that some achievement will fill the space within you, you need to make the commitment to let go of desiring and grasping, to be at peace, in a state of surrender, understanding that everything is in the hands of something higher anyway.

Human beings are constantly busy, busy, busy papering over the space in themselves, but that void is the most powerful condition of our existence. It is in that void that stillness and peace lie. It is not a scary place. That void is Infinite Uncertainty, yes, but embracing Infinite Uncertainty is the key, amazingly enough, to choosing happiness and to living beyond anxiety. This unpredictable thing that makes people anxious and want to run is actually what you'll learn to—and want to—embrace as we go along in this book. The reality of the human condition is that it is uncertain, that despite our illusions of running the show, we do not, and our surrender to ultimate Reality—in other words, to the Creative Energy that made the universe—is what allows us to stop our striving and worrying, to live at the top of the pendulum, to be perfectly still deep within ourselves. That stillness is joy.

Infinite Uncertainty is ultimate Reality; fighting that fact is precisely what leads to unhappiness.

So while you're thinking about your life as a pendulum, remember what we've established so far: You may not have control over the pendulum, but you do have control over something equally important—where you choose to live on the pendulum. And the first step toward articulating that choice is to make a firm commitment to travel light and happy, from the stillpoint inside you, having consciously let go, as you did on the swing, of your personal busy-ness.

You may not have control over life's ups and downs, but you do have a choice as to how those ups and downs will affect you. Everything you need to be truly happy and to live beyond anxiety is already inside you—everything.

INNER VISION

The Self Has No Problem

A DEEPER VISION of ourselves is necessary if we want to stop living on the arm of the pendulum, if we want to live, instead, at the stillpoint inside ourselves, beyond anxiety and unhappiness. Inner work is the conscious choice we make to pursue that deeper vision of ourselves. But there is no cookbook for inner work, no cut-and-dried success formula for reaching that stillpoint. Anyone who tells you there is, in my opinion, is feeding you something you don't want to eat. There are things you can do to climb up the arm of the pendulum in order to find that the stillness is inside yourself—and we will discuss many of them in this book—but there is no simple, neat recipe card to follow for guaranteed results.

A vision doesn't happen in a flash. It may reveal itself in a flash, but it doesn't develop in a flash. It is work: It must bake, it takes time, it takes energy, it takes a deep internalization of your attention. Above all, it takes commitment, a commitment to yourself that you will not be limited by a world defined by disease, death, decay, by this body, this mind, by the petty desires of this body, this mind. Then, the beginning of some inspiration can coalesce. Without an authentic commitment, there is little chance you will develop a center strong enough to sustain any serious work you may choose to do.

As we participate in the various educational and training programs we encounter in life, we may ask ourselves, "What will I do with my life? It's too hard for me to be a doctor or a lawyer, so I'll be an auto mechanic or a waitress." This is not to disparage auto mechanics or waitresses; depending upon what comes naturally to you, I could just as easily reverse the professions and say, "It's too hard to be an auto mechanic, I think I'll be a lawyer." The point is not what you *think* you are; the point is to turn your back on what you think you are—on fixed notions, your own or those imposed on you from outside yourself. The point is not to be afraid of doing what is hard. Embrace what does not come naturally. Only in this way will you stop limiting yourself and allow for the deepest part of you to express itself in ways you may not have imagined just yet.

I think every one of my high school counselors tried to limit me by saying I should work only with my hands. Well, I do, but in a much more profound and creative way than they ever dreamed of.

Initially, you may need to think in terms of what you *don't* want your life to be, what you don't want to limit you, rather than what you do want. You may pick some things you'd like to try, and the first thing you'll learn from that is what you don't like. You may spend ten years doing that, but if you learn from it, you're way ahead. Then, for the next ten years, you find out what you *do* like and what you *do* care about and develop your skills there. But you'll never get past what you don't like into what you do without a deeper inner vision. Why? Because plans without vision are not based on our awareness of our true potential. They are based, instead, on our fears of what we can't do and on our conditioning about what we're not. Such plans will only dissatisfy.

Plan on being the best person you can be, on tearing down every limitation you've been handed. Choose a life that is completely different from one in which you are at the mercy of this swing and that sway of the pendulum, this biological contingency and that psychological twist and turn. Choose a life of inner growth.

Life is painful no matter how you live it. There is a big dose of pain in it for everybody. To me, it's better to experience pain in the process of living something passionately and joyfully, learning and growing, than it is to endure pain in the course of being bored to death and complacently brutalized. To be happy, you must choose to be happy; you must do the work to be happy, the inner work; and a life of inner work is what we call a spiritual life.

The term "spiritual" is often loaded in our Western culture, and unfavorably so, because we have it confused with religion, with a list of "do's" and "don'ts." So when I say, choosing to be happy is tantamount to choosing to live a spiritual life, you may balk at first. But that is only because you may not, as yet, have a true understanding of what "spiritual" is.

As I mentioned earlier, a spiritual life is not one in which you renounce the world, wear special clothes, give up this thing and that thing in order to be holy. All of that is religion, and I make a sharp distinction between the religion business and a spiritual life. Religion is full of dogma and regulations, in other words, full of those limitations we've been speaking of; spirituality is formless, existing in no particular place or time, capable of transforming us endlessly and profoundly. It wears no particular clothing, eats no particular food, practices no particular ascetic hardship; it is not the province of any one people over another.

In other words, a spiritual life is not just for nuns, priests, and mystics. My teacher, Swami Rudrananda, Rudi, was a person of amazing and wonderful contradictions. He was deeply steeped in Indian culture and had been going to India since the late 1950s, yet I remember that first week I began studying with him in New York in the early 1970s, he closed his Oriental art store after a full day's work, walked over to the Second Avenue Deli, got a couple of hot dogs with sauerkraut and a lemonade, ate and drank it all, and entered meditation class as he was wiping mustard off his face with his kurta.

My teacher wasn't shackled by convention or expectation. He was himself, always. And he was deeply, deeply spiritual.

A spiritual life is available to everyone. It can be enjoyed by everyone, enrich the life of anyone. It is not, as we can see in the example of my teacher, about renunciation or self-castigation—quite to the contrary, really. It is for anyone, with this one caveat: You have to be a person who is willing to lose limitations because in a spiritual life, that's all you will lose—your limitations, your petty ideas about what you or anyone and anything should and shouldn't be. A spiritual life is not about renouncing your money or your lifestyle or your family or whatever—you don't have to whack any relationships, you don't have to change anything in particular. Those things may change or they may not; you will have choices as you grow. But, absolutely, you will lose the tiny notion you have of yourself and the world, and then what your life will become is vaster than anything that tiny notion can possibly imagine now.

To put it another way, a spiritual life is simply the opposite of a life of desire. It is not about "do's" and "don'ts" and renunciation; the concepts of calmness and virtue, which we will discuss later and which play an important part in the choice to be happy, are not about not doing something. The real issue is not renunciation. The real issue is desire and the recognition that there is no end to it and that nothing can ever fulfill it.

So what you do instead is move your desire along to the top of the pendulum, attach it to the highest state available to a person, to a deeper inner vision of your-self, of everyone and everything around you. Desire that. Strive for that. Then you have a chance for real happi-ness. That state will finish all desire, and in that state, you will see the real issue, which is not one of self-recrimination and denial, but one of where to invest your energy. Are there better places to invest it than others? Absolutely.

As we get older, we tend to think our choices are defined by age and past experience; we paint ourselves into a corner. But it's important to break out of those corners and think about what we want in life, in our heart of hearts, deeply. This wanting is not the same as desire. This is a longing to be free of the anxieties sur-rounding desire, and this freedom is our natural state.

You are completely free at all times. Completely. Only your mind and its entanglements tell you that you are not. Think again. Look again. For the most part, there is no circumstance in which you have to exist, nothing you have to do.

I am aware that for some people, brutality, poverty, illness are the norm, and rising above the violence of such lives is extremely difficult. But it is often possible. It may be hard, hard work, but it is possible because an extraordinary potential exists in each and every one of us regardless of what we've been dealt in life.

Also, the vast majority of us in this culture are fortunate in our lives. We do not live without pain—as I said before, no one does—but we are privileged. Travel to other countries, to India or Bosnia. Believe me, we are the most fortunate people on the face of the earth. So if we look at our lives honestly, we can see that the life we complain about is often the life we ourselves have made, and the people in that life are our own choices. Everyone is completely free, and what we are doing with our lives is, for the most part, what we've chosen to do—perhaps unwisely, but nonetheless, we have chosen.

So because you have chosen, live your life with love, with integrity, with energy. Otherwise, change what you're doing with your life.

Abhinavagupta, the preeminent, tenth-century Indian commentator on the Trika tradition in yoga, has written lines which sum up the truth of our state: "From the perspective of The Absolute Reality, there is no cycle of rebirth. Why, then, is there a question of shackles for living beings? The free being has never had shackles, and so to attempt to liberate him is useless. It is only an illusion, like the imaginary shadow of a demon or the rope mistaken for a serpent, which produces such unfounded confusion. Leave nothing, take nothing, and established within yourself, just as you are, happily pass the time."

All of us are intrinsically "free beings." The choice we make when we choose to be happy, when we choose a life of inner work, is simply a recognition of "The Absolute Reality," of the way things truly are—of our inherent freedom. That is the inner vision we need to cultivate, a vision of things as they truly are. The pendulum of desire, the "cycle of rebirth" is the "illusion." We amass so many layers of tension swinging around on the pendulum, wanting this and grabbing for that and coming up frustrated most of the time, we forget our true state of freedom.

But we can make a choice to release tensions every day and allow our creative energy to flow. And that is what inner work is, that is what a spiritual life is, that is what choosing to be happy is. In effect, then, isn't a spiritual life the only way to live because it is the only thing that brings us to a true understanding of what we—and all the people and things around us—really are?

Even though there is no cookbook for inner growth, it does demand some discipline. It's not a magic ceremony that someone outside ourselves performs while we sit around eating sweets and watching TV. It's work. It has some requirements and encompasses sacrifices as well as benefits. Intense sacrifices. Powerful benefits. But for me, there is no other way because swinging around on the arm of the pendulum doesn't interest me.

I cannot say this enough: To a great degree, you choose your life's path. If you aren't consciously making your own life by recognizing your choices and creating from within yourself that which you really want, then you are accepting whatever scrap of a life is available to you from the leftover resources of everybody else's struggle within the environment. You have to be clear and focused on what you want. Every single day, you have to choose to feed the deeper Life inside yourself, the deeper vision of yourself and everything around you; you have to allow it to challenge the assumptions you make about yourself—that you can or can't be this or that, that you must or must not have that or this, and so on. If you do not act out your values and refine your chosen vision every day, nothing will happen. Then, the notion of choosing happiness becomes just another pipe dream that you had.

I am being purposely vague about the exact nature of this deeper vision of yourself. If I tell you, "It is this, this, and this—*this* is your vision," I have limited you just like everybody else. Every person—*every* person—is different and individual, and there isn't just one way, there are a billion ways, there isn't just one vision, there are a bizillion. As I said earlier, there is no cookbook. How many ways are there to be quiet? There's one and a billion at the same time. How many ways to open your heart and be loving to those around you? One way—that's to open your heart and be loving, just do it—but still, different for everybody.

I will say concretely, though, that a deeper inner vision is not the same as a vision of yourself fifty pounds lighter, having a great hair day, winning friends and influencing people. Most people are struggling and struggling to improve this and that, to have a better smile, cleaner teeth, fresher breath. Ultimately, it's a big waste of time.

Inner vision has nothing to do with self-improvement, which is just more tension about the most superficial part of you. In fact, self-help is reactionary—you are reacting to something on the surface of you, hoping that by making a change there, the deep, inner pain will go away.

But what happens instead? People who lose weight often regain it; dye jobs wreck hair; face lifts don't last, neither does fresh breath; and therapy, while it attempts to reach the depths of our dissatisfactions in order to dissolve them, winds up feeding them as we talk and talk about them until they have so much energy in them, they become more powerful, more hypnotic, more absolutely entrenched in our psyches than they ever were before. The final clunker is, we may have done all this for our boyfriend or wife, and suddenly they decide they like fat, bald, sagging, and neurotic.

Self-improvement is like the old Arabic saying of putting five fingers on five fleas: You may get four of them, but in trying to get the fifth, you will lose the whole thing and have to start over again. It's an endless struggle. Self-improvement is our response to the stress, strain and trauma we experience growing up. We try to free ourselves from these strains, but like the material desire from which self-help springs, self-help is just another tension, another source of frustration, another need we can't ultimately satisfy.

It *is* a beginning, though. Self-help is on a continuum with inner vision because it, too, is about change. Reacting to something on the surface of you in order to effect a deep change is as good a place as any to start making the shift in your old patterns which will allow for greater happiness in your life. But to end up somewhere extraordinary, in a place inside yourself where you are deeply happy, you have to rise above the whole notion of self-help.

We are all part of a technological age, trained to think that we can solve any problem. We have identified pain as a problem, so we must solve it. This is where self-improvement begins to look attractive. But, as we said earlier, pain is not a problem, and therefore, it is impossible to solve. Pain is simply a natural part of the experience of change and growth—the experience of being alive.

Walk outside and look at a tree with a few years growth on it. The bark is probably scarred, with ridges and eccentricities that are completely natural to it. The scars are natural. Pain is natural. The scars, the pain are simply part of the tree being alive.

Pain is not a problem; our inability to deal with it may be a problem, but pain itself is not a problem. So, having said that, then a deeper inner vision means that you cut through, reach through, the conditioning that says that you are this thing or that thing, that you can or can't do this or that, that you have to please your parents or whomever, that you need to have that and this in order to be happy. You reach past all issues of limitation, of problem—pain or otherwise—to the deepest part of yourself, and you stay there, stay connected to that limitless depth, to the place where you are authentic and real and true and in touch with yourself. Stay there, until your creative energy becomes strong enough to manifest a vision of how it wants to express itself through you.

Then you know what you want to do with this life, you understand that it doesn't have much to do with superficial change—although you may indulge in that from time to time. You appreciate yourself and your life as they exist right now. Then it is possible for you, as Abhinavagupta said, "just as you are, happily (to) pass the time."

The essence of fulfillment in life is to have a deep inner vision of how to be a vehicle for something much higher and finer than the world of desires. That vision is satisfying and joyful. But the part of you that serves that vision is not the you with which you've become familiar.

As I said earlier, most of us define ourselves in very limited ways. This self with which we identify has all kinds of boundaries. We say that it has a certain hair and eye color, talents in this or that direction; it has gender roles and financial responsibilities; it likes this food or clothing and dislikes that; is allergic, well, ill. We insist on quantifying and coding it.

Above all, we unanimously agree, this tiny self has lots of problems. It has this hair color and wants that, it is ill and must be well, it can't do that job—and, oh, yes, it can't do that one either. The little self is full of anxieties and problems; it is the product of trauma, stress, and strain.

Now, back up for a minute and think of that higher and finer Power we spoke of in Chapter One. As we said before, that Power is in control of our lives, and the beginning of our choice to be happy is to surrender to that ultimate Reality because It simply is the truth about our condition as human beings. We *are* surrendered to something higher and finer at all times anyway, whether we acknowledge this truth or not. Surrendering to It consciously is part of our choice to be happy.

Do you think that fundamental Power has problems? It's laughable to think that It does. So tell me, if the Power that gives you life has no problem, if the Creator of your innermost being has no problem, if your essence, the Vital Force in you, has no problem, do *you* have a problem? Maybe your little self *thinks* you do, but your big Self *knows* It doesn't.

Take a moment and look beyond the external part of you. Feel deeply into yourself; close your eyes and feel into a more profound part of you. Take a few minutes and reach deep, deep into the core of you.

Open your eyes. Isn't the depth you contacted different from the level on which you may be used to operating? That depth is the Self, with a capital "S;" it is the essence of you that is God.

For a moment, imagine living only from that big Self, from Self-expression, not self-expression. What do you find? First, automatically, you are at the top of the pendulum, at the stillpoint, above the swings and sways of desire. You are living from someplace much bigger than the little corner you've painted yourself into your whole life. In this place, there are no boundaries. From this place, we understand that the things or people which limit our time, our energy, our sense of well-being have come from poor choices and not from anything intrinsic to our state, which is naturally one of boundlessness and freedom— of happiness.

And here is the wonder of it: The big Self can even find nourishment in the challenges presented by the little self's choices. The tensions generated by those choices— which are usually motivated by a concern for "What's going to happen to little, ol' me?"—may seem to be a reason for us to have some sense of limitation, frustration, disappointment. We will discuss this in much greater detail later, but in truth, when you take all the energy of all the choices and all the ways in which you express yourself and share your life—both simple and demanding—if you take it all deeply into your Self as food, and if you strive in all circumstances, whether easy or difficult, to manifest fineness and quality—in other words, if you really give love when it's both hard and easy—then everything promotes your growth, your freedom, and your sense of happiness and well-being. Everything promotes your sense of Self.

From this vantage point, self-improvement becomes a non-existent issue because if your essence has no problem, what are you going to improve exactly? You are above the whole notion of self-help because you see clearly that you don't need help. Your little self may need help from time to time, we all need help. But I'm talking about this in the deepest sense, and when you live from that deep place, in contact with that authentic, deeper

Self, you are above self-help because you are above the idea that you need help—you are above the self.

Then, we don't say, "Oh, I am this or that. I am feeling this thing or that thing." We don't have the idea we have a problem because we're living from that place within ourselves that is the Self, with a capital "S," and the Self has no problem.

When you live from the Self, everything is enjoyable. Whether the little self is well or sick, depressed or anxious, the Self is always well, always full of joy. I'm sure there have been times when you were in some beautiful place—the scenery was spectacular; maybe it was a moody mountain landscape or a sunny seashore. It doesn't matter. It was beautiful; you knew at the time it was beautiful. But you were too depressed or anxious and couldn't feel the beauty of it. If at that point, you had known how to contact the Self and reach through the depressed and anxious tensions of the little self, you would have found the scenery thoroughly enjoyable. Then, even it were New York City at rush hour on a smoggy day, it would have been blue sky, fresh air and complete tranquility to you.

If what you think about are problems, then problem consciousness will dominate your existence. But if you reach beyond your self and continue to reach into that highest place, which is also the deepest place within you, then you are transformed, and every pattern will be dissolved.

So what do you do in order to reach past trauma and tension to the depth and vastness of the Self? How do you go about living every second of every day from that place that is both deep inside yourself and high up on the pendulum of life? The answer is simple: inner work. Practice, practice, practice.

As I said earlier, there is no one way to practice—there is no cookbook. There are mountains of books written on billions of practices and billions of people who do them, and sorry to say, rather poorly. If it were any other way, the world would be a very different place than it is.

Take any practice you want, take your pick. The key is this: If you do it deeply—with love and devotion—it will work, whatever it is. In this book, there is a chapter on meditation, on exercises which I teach students to help them release tension and allow creative energy to flow. This meditation is an excellent way to practice living from that deeper place within yourself. But if you only concentrate on techniques—and I've run across six to eight hundred of them in the last twenty years and at least forty-four thousand different mantras as well—you won't get far. Because it is the love and devotion that will transform you, not techniques per se. It is the love and devotion. It is working with love.

We talk about love and devotion in a spiritual practice, not because an authentic spiritual teacher needs that love and devotion. Believe me, an authentic teacher needs your love and devotion—or anything this world has to offer—like he or she needs another foot. In spiritual practice, love and devotion are encouraged because that's the kind of person you need to be in order to grow, in order to shift your awareness from problem consciousness to something higher and finer—in order to choose to be happy.

Don't think about your problems; think instead about the love that exists in you, and if you think about that love over and over and over and over again, that love will become so strong in you as to manifest itself in a remarkable existence. Then you will not just *think* about love, you will *feel* it.

> *If you love your life, if you accept yourself as you are, you will find that life will start loving you back, and the miracles that take place for you, and within you, will amaze you. You worry about what you are and what you're not; you worry about all kinds of things. Forget it. Forget it all. Accept yourself just as you are because the idea that anybody is worth knowing just because of something they possess—some quality or thing—has nothing to do with anything that is real in Life.*

Your life may be brutal; life for all of us is not easy, even though, as I said earlier, we, in this culture, are fortunate. But no matter how difficult your life is, work to love it. Work hard to love it. That's the work—to love your life, yourself, everyone, and everything, just as they are. The real practice is to love your life. Get up every morning and appreciate your life; try to think about what you wish to grow to be. Is what you're currently doing really expressing that? It's for you to decide. Then go out and walk the walk, and talk the talk, and do it and be it. That's the real thing.

There's hard work in the middle. You do have to be willing to work. But anyone who is willing can do this work. Believe me, there is no one who is smart enough or pretty enough or rich enough to qualify; only willingness qualifies a person. As I said before, there is no quality you can possess that will make you worth knowing—just your willingness to live from the deepest part of you, however that may manifest.

So forget everything you think you're not. Having a deep inner vision, choosing to be happy, has at the foundation you—just as you are—sick, well, cute, whatever. You—loving your life, warts, stripes, and all.

THE WISH TO GROW

Opening Your Heart,

Loving Your Life

*T*HE THERAVADA BUDDHISTS from Ceylon and Thailand have as part of their practice asking the question three times a day, "Why was I born?" We all ask: "What am I doing here, why was I born? What is the meaning of my existence?" The answer is simple: "We are growing." The meaning of life is that simple— we are here to grow.

I think most people are afraid that life may be about dying, not about growing or anything that sounds interesting or pleasant. When pressed, all of our issues—all of the problems the little self thinks it has—come down to one thing: death. The desires we reach for so frenetically —the money we absolutely have to make, the relationships we think we can't live without—are just ways we distract ourselves from one central fact: We are dying from the moment we are born, and at some point, each and every one of us will no longer be here.

We cannot shy away from this point. The fact of death is something we all need to face in order to live. Death is going to happen. It is going to happen. And guess what? It's not going to happen when and how we want it—the entire event is completely up to God. Saying this may not make me popular, but saying this is the truth. Ultimate Reality is Infinite Uncertainty. Uncertainty is what is real. Our grabbing for security in this thing and that thing—in relationships, finances, obsessions with self-improvement— that is the illusion. So we can either get hysterical and worry away our earthly existence about the fact that we and everyone and everything around us are going to per- ish, or we can come to a deeper understanding of the meaning of existence.

If we are not afraid to die, then we are not afraid to live. Then we are free.

The bottom-line problem we feel we have is death. But here is the wonderful thing about this problem: Only the little self identifies with it. The big Self knows there is no problem, even with something as potentially terrifying as death. Why?

Because the big Self is already with God; It knows It is of God. The big Self has no problem dying and joining God because the big Self is already there.

It is important that you understand this because only if you clear up your misunderstanding can you reach through the veil of your tensions in order to feel your creative energy, to live from the Self and be happy. You cannot reach through tensions if at the core of your life is this major tension about death. Cutting through tensions means reaching through your little self, with all its wants and desires—which are only tension, that is all desire is, just tension—to access the bigger Self, which is the Vital Force, God, Creative Energy, whatever you choose to call it, within you.

God is in you. God is not something outside yourself.

So you have a choice in life: You can either live with your problems or live with God. To translate, you can either live entangled in the world of the little self, or you can see through the veil of the self's desires and allow your life to be an expression of the higher, finer, and bigger part of you that is God and has no problems. It's up to you. It's not really a tough choice to make; after all, if your life isn't the happiest event at the moment, it probably has been brought to you by a grant from the little self.

There are no such things as problems, only tensions. There is no such thing as bad and good, only tension and tension-free. Everything that happens and your reaction to it come down to this: Are you going to get tense about it or are you going to use the energy of the event to grow? When you understand that there are no problems you have to solve in your life, just tensions you must cut through, then you understand that whatever it is you think is an issue can be dropped in a flash—without thinking about it and talking about it and looking at it this way and that. It's just tension—reach through it, absorb it, digest it—drop it.

There are no such things as good and bad energies—there is only Energy, and with a little practice, all of It can be used as food for your growth.

So here's the bottom line: Life is only about death if you make it that way. If you live from the little self, life will definitely look like death because life will only be about desire, about your small self. All of the things we desire, and the little self that clings to those desires, are completely subject to decay and death. Completely. So if your desires are what you're attached to, then the things you do in life will always have some kind of death in them. As the fifteenth-century poet, Kabir, has put it, there will always be some kind of "weird failure" in everything you do.

The little self is the only thing about us that dies. The little self loses all of its self in death. But we're not at war with our small selves. This is not a dualistic universe—everything is one thing. We will discuss this in greater detail later, but for now, let me say that your body is simply a condensation of energy. It hasn't condensed here in this form for you to fight with it. You may have to rise above its concerns often, but as long as you can manage those concerns, everything will be fine. Enjoy what your body wants to enjoy; smell, taste, feel everything; but be aware that the life of the little self is not Life Itself.

The Self, with a big "S," is of Vital Force, Creative Energy, God; and that Energy has no end; and It knows it. In meditation, in deep prayer, in whatever practice you choose to do, what you're doing is reaching through the tensions, the little self, to that part of you that has no misunderstanding, that knows where It comes from and what It is doing here. You live, then, from that place. From that state, you know that Life is about growing, not about desire and death. You understand that if you live your life as an expression of love, then you live a life that is full of joy. When you choose to live from your Self, you choose to be happy.

❀

When I teach meditation, I suggest that students hold in their hearts a deep wish to grow. The wish to grow becomes their mantra for a time.

But what is growth? If that's what we're all doing here—growing—why do we have to ask for it? Doesn't it just happen?

Growing is what we're doing here, yes, but our entanglements in the tensions we allow ourselves in our daily lives limit our growth, sometimes severely. As long as desire rules us, our growth will be stunted at best. Often, we have the ability to rationalize and justify our desires. "My desires are different," we may say. "My desires are on a higher plane. I'm not clinging to this relationship or this money for myself. I'm in the relationship for the other person. I need the money for my family, not for myself."

Unless the only desire you have is your wish to grow, your desires are no different from anyone else's. What you desire is really a function of the depth that you're in contact with inside of you, so if your deepest contact is with the Self, then your main desire will be to grow.

Ultimately, though, it is necessary to surrender all desire, even your wish to grow, and to allow your life to flow as an expression of the deepest part of you. Again, though, remember that surrendering desire, worldly or otherwise, does not mean renouncing the world, living the life of a nun or an aesthete. I live in the world, you live in the world. We just do live in the world, and we are not here to deny anything.

But we are here to live from the Self, and that means we are here to express the God in us, the Vital Force, the Creative Energy. And the best way we can serve God is by focusing on growing.

Growth has nothing to do with "me, me, me, me." Growth happens as the "me," the little self, dissolves. Growth is the dissolution of "I need, I want, I have to have." You grow by making your life an expression of real love.

Notice, I said "real" love. By this, I do not mean romance. Romance, as exhilarating as it may be for a time, is about, to put it bluntly but truthfully, hormones. Isn't it the case that we often say we "love" somebody when we really don't know them at all? What we mean by love in those instances is attraction. It's nice, to be sure, and sometimes when you are attracted to somebody, the relationship grows, you come to respect that person, and that respect leads to real love—love without self-interest, love where you're not constantly looking for what you're going to get out of it. But this is rare. Romance is not real love; there's too much desire in romance, especially in the beginning, for it to be a disinterested event.

Real love has no agenda; it's not *your* agenda. It's like true friendship; a real friend is someone who puts aside their interests for the sake of the highest best interest of the relationship. Even when it's unpleasant or difficult or doesn't fit in with their plans, a true friend is there for you. Sometimes, a friend is tough with you and won't assist you in your entanglements and tensions, even if you turn on your friend for a time as a result. In other words, a true friend is willing to let go of short-term gain for your long-term best interest. This is real love.

When you open your heart and consistently express love for everyone and everything in your environment, you grow. It's by focusing on what love is and trying your best to act it out, even if you don't always do a supremely fabulous job, that you become a very big person. It is loving that leads to love; it is being willing to take the risk and, on occasion, to deal with the pain of loving that brings love.

It is by loving that love grows.

Again, there's no cookbook for this. What you look like as a loving person may be different from what I look like as a loving person and so on. Just reach into your heart and be the most loving person you can be. Just do it. Sometimes, if you have to take in poison, do so, and give back love. Then, whatever the face of love is, it will be your face.

A loving person is a growing person. That's because a loving person is an open person, and it is impossible to be tense and truly open or loving at the same time. I said earlier that there is no such thing as good and bad, only tension and tension-free. Let's take that one step further. There is no such thing as good and bad, only tension and love. When I say that you must release tension and allow your creative energy to flow, that is the same as my saying, You are here to grow, which is the same as saying, You are here to love, which is also, You are here to serve Life Itself. It is also the same thing as, Open your heart, love your life. First and foremost, be a loving person because that is the same as being a growing person. It is all one thing: growing, loving, serving, releasing tension, flow, opening your heart, loving your life. And it begins with surrender, with your recognition that God is in the driver's seat, not you. It begins with an open heart.

But what exactly do I mean by "open heart?" Think back to the love without self-interest that we spoke of earlier. You may have felt this kind of love for your children, for a parent or a teacher, for that true friend we referred to before—whomever, whatever.

When I first met my teacher, Rudi, I took one look at him, and my heart shattered with love.

You may remember that when you had that feeling of love without an agenda, there was also a feeling of expansion in your chest, a sweetness—a love—in the center of your chest. Your heart felt as if it were open to the point of bursting.

And here's the amazing thing: You can consciously choose every single day—every single moment of every single day—to open yourself up to yourself and to your life just the way that child or mentor or friend or circumstance unwittingly opened you up before. You can open your heart and love your life—by choice. You can do it for yourself; it just takes a little practice. Then, you don't have to wait for some random accident outside yourself to make you feel open and loving. You can do it for yourself. By breathing and opening your heart.

In a way, having a wish to grow is simply a mechanism for creating a constant reminder within yourself to breathe—not to think, to breathe—and to feel your breath and the flow of vitality within you as you breathe. Breath is the mechanism by which you know you are alive. Observe your breath, and then observe the source and the extension of that flow of vitality. To follow your breath is to go deeper and deeper inside yourself to the source of Life. To do so takes you beyond experience, beyond mind, beyond the little self to the Self. In the awareness of breath, in the awareness of the source of Life, you are at peace.

The key here, however, is that you are not opening your heart to anything outside yourself. You are opening your heart to your Self. The only thing to hold onto in this whole life is in you right now, was always in you, and is ever in you. It is to go to that place and stay there that is the essence of growth. You begin to choose to be happy and love your life by opening your heart—to you. The essence of you, your innermost Self, is the source of all of

Life. Therefore, when you open your heart to your deepest Self, you are automatically opening to everything in life—the things you like and the things you don't—and to something higher and finer as well. When you take your attention through your small self to your essential Self, reaching through your individual tensions, veils, and worries, this reaching becomes a mechanism by which you grow, by which you can give love to this life and to the people in it, even when you may not be liking it or them very much at that moment.

You don't have to like everything in your life in order to choose to be happy; you just have to open your heart and love it.

Your life does not come from outside you, your life flows from within. The opportunities you have, the people you meet, the connections you establish or don't establish, the way in which you see people and circumstances that allow you to find something of benefit or nothing of benefit in them flow from within you. It has nothing to do with anything or anyone else. Yes, there is a Creative Power, Vital Force, God that has breathed Life into you, but *you are* Vital Force, *everything is* Vital Force. There is no separation between you, the Power that made you, and the extraordinary Creative Energy that lies within you. None.

You can search the whole wide world, search it over and over, and not find the things which will bring you ease and comfort and the experience of fulfillment in your life because, in fact, that only flows from within you. This feeling of joy will not, in any way, be dependent upon money or someone else loving you first. What it is dependent upon, totally, is your contact with your Self. Your openness with and within you. Your flow within *you*.

So now some of you may be thinking, "This is all very fine for him to say. He's been practicing inner work for years, he probably doesn't have any real problems, so that's why he thinks we can be happy and love everybody all the time. But I can't. I'm sick, I'm married to a person who treats me terribly. I'm so depressed or so anxious or so something that I can't even find my heart, let alone open it. What love? What life? And what does he mean: I don't have to 'like' my life, I 'just have to love it?' 'Just love it!' That's the hardest thing of all! I don't think that's possible."

I can't argue with you; I won't argue with you. I can tell you this thing and that thing about my life to prove that I have had, and do have, my share of difficulty, but then that would become a contest over problems. And as I said before, problem consciousness does not interest me because it has nothing to do with things as they *really* are, things as they are deeply inside you. Deeply inside you, everything is well.

I can only tell you this: If you work every single day with as much love for the sometimes difficult people you deal with—including yourself—as you can muster in that anxious, depressed, or whatever heart of yours, your entire nervous system, your body chemistry, will change completely. The secret to transformation, pure and simple, is to work with love in dealing with everyone and everything—and this includes dealing with yourself, too. It takes practice and it takes time, but it works. Transformation will happen for you, but you are the one who has to make it happen.

You took a lifetime to get gummed up. There is no quick fix. But you can begin by dropping every excuse —no matter how good it sounds now—as to why you can't do anything about this mess your life seems to be at the moment.

You think you're frozen or depressed or anxious—so anxious, you're convinced you can't sit long enough to access the stillness within you? This is the result of years of self-abuse. It takes a long time to get rigid and crazed. But not to worry. All of that can melt. If you just keep opening your heart and stay with that—breathe into that —you will feel a simple joy. You may only be able to do it for three minutes today and not at all tomorrow. Keep trying. Don't beat yourself up. Do it as many times as you can every day for as long as you can. Eventually, your life will be lived from that stillpoint we spoke of earlier; your whole life will be an expression of a dynamic stillness.

From your current state of mind, you may not be able to paint a picture of the potential which exists within you for growing and for benefiting everyone around you—even the people who seem to be a trial for you. Each and every human being on the face of this earth has the same extraordinary potential locked within him or her. That potential is not to make money—although that may happen—or to find a mate—even though that may happen, too—or whatever your pet desire is at the moment. The potential I am speaking about is to be completely happy, to enjoy at all times a profound sense of well-being.

But you have to stop keeping score; you have to put away your regular accounting system: "I did *this* for them so they have to do *that* for me." We're not in this world functioning and sharing and giving to get something back. It's more productive to be in this world loving to love—because when we start to love, when we start to share, it's exhausting sometimes, yes, but the bottom line is: When we put out, we get back, period. The minute we rise above the level of the faces—"I'll put down my weapons when they put down theirs"—then what we do over here comes back over there. There is a flow, and it may not come back to us in the way we want—rarely does it come back in the same direction in which we put it out because it is a flow—but it does come back.

Open your mind, your heart, your eyes to living, and simply live, love, share.

Let me make this a bit more concrete. You're listening to me tell you to love your life, and you're still saying, "I can't do that. My life is too hard. The jerks are too jerky." In the chapter on meditation in this book, we'll deal with specific things you can do everyday to melt tension and allow creative energy to flow. But for right now, just briefly, instead of saying, "I can't love my life," take a deep breath, lightly, don't strain, and then take another one. Now try opening your heart.

Do that every time you want to say, "I can't."

Then, think of facing the people who are less than supportive of you. Open your heart and stop judging them. Understand one very crucial aspect of ultimate Reality, and I cannot overemphasize how important this point is: Every human being, no matter what kind of an awful person you think they are, *every* human being is a manifestation of Vital Force. Every person derives his or her own life from the same source as your own, and on that basis alone, every person deserves your respect.

The first thing I do in dealing with people, whether they've been wonderful or less-than-wonderful to me, is to clear my mind of my past experience with them and of any preconceived notions I have about the circumstances under discussion. I clear my mind and myself of my tensions and any issues, and I start to work from the flow to a caring and a compassion for whatever it is that I'm relating to; then, I try to understand what the best outcome for that situation would be, and I encourage everyone to take little steps in that direction.

But in your dealings with people and with yourself, while you may be compassionate, you mustn't suppress, repress, or deny anything. Wrestle with your fear and pain; don't pretend anything. Don't fawn over the brutes or fake tenderness for brutality. Facing these things on the front side is far better than trying to push them down. But the best thing is to see beyond all of it. The real transformation in you comes when you can give love in exchange for poison.

The dynamic in your life changes when you start being grateful for the life you have, when you stop feeding the fear and pain—the problem consciousness.

It's not appropriate to suppress any feelings, but it also doesn't get you anywhere to engage in them. Feelings are often hormone-based, they're chemistry, and as such, they can be very misleading. Don't deny them, but don't get entangled in them either. When various feelings arise, see them for what they are: products of body chemistry, not deep psychological mysteries. If you demystify your feelings, then the ones you find so torturous will, like a wave, come and go. You won't push them under, you won't be thrown around by them, you will simply note them and move on.

All feelings can be classified as either feelings about others or feelings about ourselves, but no matter what the classification, all feelings come down to one thing: What's going to happen to me? The next time you have a strong feeling, check it out. Isn't the basis of the fear, jealousy, anger, desire, or longing: I'm afraid because I don't know what's going to happen to me in this; or I'm jealous because I don't know what's going to happen to me; I really want that person to "love" me, and I say I "love" them, because I don't know what's going to happen to me; and so on? Be honest. Your absorption with your body chemistry is what's behind most of the feelings you think are so important and that you allow to rule your life.

Struggling with our feelings is the province of the little self, and we've already established that we can't live from that place and have the one feeling that doesn't come from our chemistries—the feeling of total well-being we get when we live more and more from the Self, from a place of real love—the feeling that arises every time we choose to open our hearts.

The quality of our lives is much more dependent on the quality of love we have for our lives than it is on the quality of love other people have for us.

If you understand this, then everything productive will take place—not necessarily everything you want, but definitely everything you need to become the finest person you can possibly be.

If you're looking for somebody else to do something for you, then you'll be miserable because, as we've already established, the quality of your life rests with you, with the love you bring to that life. If you're searching for anything outside yourself to fill some hole you think you have, then you'll probably be searching for a very, very, very, very, very, very, very long time. And you won't find what you're looking for.

It is for each of us, it is *on* us, to do the work inside ourselves that is necessary to love our lives. If you look to yourself in each situation and with every person you meet, look to yourself to bring up from within you the quality of love you hope to share with other people, then that love will be there for you, too. In time, that love will become very powerful within you. It will transform the whole field of your experience, and the only thing you need do is to try not to make unnecessary tensions in your life. If you try not to make unnecessary tensions with anybody, and within yourself, try not to harbor unnecessary tensions, then *nothing* can keep your love down—nothing.

As a Catholic growing up, I was raised to love the sinner but hate the sin. I like that idea. It is unfortunate, just ridiculous and brutal, how people behave and are often forced to behave by life. Respect them anyway. They're probably surprised themselves that they're behaving like that.

But just because you respect somebody does not mean you allow them to defecate in your living room. If they do, don't invite them back. You don't have to; as we said before, you're free in every way. It's possible to say, "No," and keep your heart completely open. Open your heart and respect the person, respect the creative energy flowing within them, even if it's not manifesting very productively at the moment.

The Buddhists use the term, "compassion;" they speak of having compassion for every living being. It is because everyone is fundamentally a manifestation of Life that you must respect him or her first, and from that respect, compassion arises. Here is a person who has the same deep inner power you have, and regardless of how they got into a mess, you have to feel compassion.

If it's possible to help this person, you might, although first, deeply connect within yourself, live from that place deep inside yourself, so that you don't become entangled in another person's tensions. It's hard enough to be responsible for yourself; you must be careful when miring yourself in some responsibility you think you have for someone else. If you stay in a simple place within yourself and relate to any complexity openly—but from that simple place—then any situation you're in won't magnetize you.

Stay attuned to yourself in every environment—hostile, friendly, peaceful, violent, and so on. That way, you will sustain and even expand your own center always. Train yourself and your mind to focus on this expansion, which we'll discuss in more detail later.

For now, understand that, as Rudi used to say, "Life must be consumed whole, with all its tensions and pain and joy." You want to consume life, you don't want to be consumed by the life you lead and the people in it. If you allow yourself to be consumed by every kind of tension, you're left with little inner resource for your own growth. But once you've begun to live from the Self, and if in the process of extending yourself, the person you're relating to takes to it and responds, then there's an expansion of the flow, and you've taken a situation that could have consumed you and turned it into an expression of that deep love inside you. You've digested tensions, absorbed them.

We're not here in the name of openness to avoid or deny conflict. Conflict is inevitable. It happens continuously. There's conflict inside us and between us. However, to a great degree, this conflict is resolved through our effort to absorb tensions, and our ability to absorb them is based on our capacity to respect genuinely the interests of everyone with whom we associate. If you respect those interests, then as you work with and communicate with people, you'll be looking out for their interests as well as your own.

Many discussions about problems wouldn't arise if within ourselves, we simply sat down and opened our hearts. When we have an awareness of our interconnectedness, we have the capacity, quietly and very deeply, to serve one another without saying a word. So try in yourself to feel some understanding and compassion for everybody and take care of each environment that you function in the best way you can—your own first.

In a state of openness, we respect the powers and forces and people around us because each of us is a force.

If we respect that, then we listen, we appreciate the tension in a situation, we absorb it, we grow from that process—we can't help but grow. We change ourselves internally through this exchange process. We observe our ability to take in and convert tensions, and we flow with it. Then, we can make the changes in ourselves and in our lives that are appropriate to the well-being of the total environment, not just to one person's momentary need.

Truly listening, clearly seeing—these are the beginnings of being conscious. Take tensions from the lowest level and transform them and the field around them into something higher.

In addition, demonstrate respect for other people's interests; be willing to extend yourself to serve their interests even as you contemplate ways to promote your own. This is how to create a flow. From a spiritual viewpoint, even if it costs you something, establishing and sustaining this flow is in everyone's best interest, including your own. Again, you don't have to let anybody walk all over you, but if you're living from the Self, in the Source of all things, then your actions and decisions will reflect the highest best interest of a situation and not just what you want or think you need in order to survive.

When you come from the Self, you don't become entangled in the struggles that exist among individuals in various circumstances. You understand the need for cooperation and flow within *every* situation in order that all people involved have a chance to succeed in whatever it is they're trying to do.

As you deal with the people and circumstances in your life, when you feel agitation, pain, and suffering, instead of denying or reacting, simply open. As we said before, pain, fear, and the like are not bad; they're just energy, information. They may be telling you that something isn't quite right, that some action regarding that situation may indeed be called for from you at an appropriate time and place. Sit quietly, surrender to what God wants for you in life and not what you want from God;

open your heart, love everyone and everything in the situation, and then deal with it. Don't squelch it, run away from it or duck it; don't breathe and open just to escape. Surrender, open, love, deal.

This is how you begin to love your life, yourself, and those people you think are so impossible. Open your heart to yourself, to others, and to everything in life; come from the Self in resolving the tensions of your life. Don't suppress anything. Everything is energy. Use it to grow. Love Life; grow. Then you've chosen to be happy.

If you love your life, it will definitely love you back. Maybe not the way you'd like, but it *will* love you back.

However, you have to make the first move.

Love your life, love everything and everyone in your life just as it is and just as they are—now. And this includes loving you. There's no better person you can be than the one you are right now. If you're doing your inner work, you're growing, and wherever it is you are at any given point, as a growing person, is completely fine. If you're growing, you're not going to be the same person five days from now or five weeks from now or five years from now that you are today.

Then, some of you will get married, and some of you won't. None of you will find your soul mate because there is no such thing—you are complete, just as you are. Some of you will have children, some of you won't. Some will have money, some, not. Some of you will travel, others won't. Some of you will be rocket scientists, some, not. Whatever your life is, if you live in contact with the deepest part of you, everything that comes to you will be appropriate to the Vital Force within you and to its quality and capacity for Self-expression.

The issue is not what you do in life or what your life circumstances are. The issue is who you are, and the answer to that should be: You are the finest person you can possibly be at any given moment.

"I want to be somebody else" is a thought I find percolating often in people. Sometimes, the hardest thing for many people is to be themselves. When we encounter someone we want to attract in a relationship, as a business partner, whatever, we often talk what we want to be, not who we really are. Forget it. Just be yourself. It's okay not to conform to any image; in fact, it's wonderful. What you want to promote instead of image is an authentic contact with yourself and with others that can allow for a real exchange to take place. It is in that exchange process that what we experience totally transcends what we are and makes accessible a dimension of ourselves that is truly divine. And that dimension is the Self.

Love yourself, love your life—first. Life *will* love you back. You don't have to *like* everything in your life, just love it. This is an important distinction. It's not necessary to *like* difficult people or *like* being sick or *like* being poor, or whatever the issue is. Of course you don't like it. But it's necessary, if you're going to break out of the old patterns into something extraordinary, to *love* your life, to *open* to all of the diverse circumstances of your existence.

As we said in Chapter Two, having a spiritual practice is important in your choice to be happy, but without love, your practice will disintegrate. You can't legislate love; you can't legislate respect, and when you talk about practices, disciplines, or rules, what rules will you follow that will lead to love? None. No amount of practices can take you to the highest level. Only an open heart and caring can take you there. You have to care, and you have to be willing to give of yourself, I mean really give of your Self, and if you're willing, then you'll really get back—maybe not in the way you want or imagine, but it's true—if you love your life, Life will definitely love you back.

When you turn your attention to that Source of Life within you, when you feel It and are aware of It every day, It becomes powerful and expands within you. Then you start to have a magnetism operating in your life that attracts opportunities for an increased flow in every domain. It becomes important at that stage to have your priorities well-established so you don't get swallowed up by your newfound opportunities. But for the moment, just love your life, and it will become an extraordinary one.

In everybody, a fine, deep state of understanding and a happy existence is available at all times. It's up to you to choose it; it doesn't just happen by accident. You have to choose to love your life every single day. Rudi used to say, "You can't want it one day and not the next and get it." You have to choose. If you don't, then life will choose for you, and you will probably be dealt your cards from the bottom of the deck.

You have to think over very carefully how to arrange your life so as not to have the trauma in it day after day that makes it hard to connect to the deepest part of you. It's much more important to have within yourself the experience of simple happiness than it is to have all the material benefits available in the whole universe because without peace and quiet within you, benefits do nothing but make you agitated. As we said earlier, struggling for things is the source of disease and death, not the answer to our fears about Infinite Uncertainty.

Desire is really the death of our Life.

Thinking about what Life wants of us and really working to serve our Life brings us an experience of total well-being in every dimension, not immediately, but as time passes. There's nothing that will make you happy that you don't have within you right this minute. Nothing. It's impossible that you should miss anything you really need. It's impossible. Because everything is already within you.

The important thing is that you're relaxed and happy and love your life. Love your mother and father and brothers and sisters and even the people who don't always treat you well. Love everyone with whom you've ever had and will ever have and do ever have to associate.

Love your life, not because it's objectively anything, but because it's yours. God gave it to you. Love it.

And then if every single day, you understand that meditation is just the thing you do to get in touch with, in a very pure way, that love of Life, and you allow that love to grow in you, you're going to have a life richer than you can imagine. The experience of fulfillment doesn't require looking to one thing while trying to avoid or suppress another. Just enjoy your life as it is right now. Don't think, "Oh, if only this were different, it would be better, or if that were different, I would have a better situation." Perhaps you will cut out some things that are entanglements, but understand that some stress—and a lot of imperfection—is just what life is.

Simply put, when you don't love your life just as it is—when you refuse to live from Reality, refuse to see things as they are—you starve yourself; no growth is possible. Open your heart, love your life, grow. You will be amazed at the nourishment you receive.

QUIETING THE MIND

Surrender, Calmness, and Virtue

*O*FTEN I SAY to my students, "Surrender is the key." Surrender is the key to everything, especially to unlocking the happiness within you because without surrender, you will not be able to reach through the tensions that cut you off from your true Self—from the Self that has no problems and is deeply well.

The true Self, the big Self in everyone, is calm and virtuous. No matter what form your life is taking at the moment, no matter how chaotic or messy it appears to be —and no matter how you identify yourself now: anxious, sick, well, whatever—the core of you, the core of everyone, is one thing: It is of God. It is quiet and strong. It is the part of you that expresses the highest and finest vibration of the universe. When you and everything you do expresses that vibration, no matter what your life circumstances, you are filled with joy.

But what is surrender exactly? To whom or to what do we surrender? I'll answer the second question first. Always, you are surrendering your self, with a small "s," to your Self, with a capital "S." You're not surrendering to anybody or anything outside of you. In a state of surrender, you have surrendered to your inner Self, which is far deeper, as we said before, than the self of desires, hormones, and chemistry. It is the Self that expresses God. Basically, when you surrender, you're surrendering to your own inner heart of hearts, to the highest best interest in you, to the God in you. There is only one Life Force, only one thing in life that has vitality, and is in each of us equally. And that is the essence that human beings call God.

It is very important that you understand this truth: Not even God is outside of you, is "other" than you. God is within, and so to surrender is to find that deep part within you that is of God and to live from that; in which case, the only thing you are ever surrendering is your mind and emotions, your tensions and limitations, your boundaries that say you cannot do this and that—that say, for one thing, that God is something way up there or way out there to which you beg, every now and then, to get what you want.

It is surrender that allows a bigger person to emerge and to replace the smaller person you used to be, and this will happen over and over and over and over again as you grow. By surrendering to that higher Force within you, you are releasing all tensions and allowing your creative energy to express itself.

One crucial limitation you must surrender in your choice to be happy is your personal history. Your past is one of the biggest tensions you carry around with you. Why? First, because it's almost entirely a product of the mind. To be sure, events do have a factual basis, but the way most of us remember them—which is what matters since we create our reactions from these memories—is often largely false.

Have you ever noticed how shoddy a piece of equipment human memory is? I'll be talking with four or five of my closest friends, friends whom I've known for twenty years or more; we'll be discussing an event, and few, if any of us, will have the same memories of it. We can barely agree on when or where it happened, let alone what happened exactly or how we felt about it. Everyone does this; human beings base their future actions on circumstances which no longer exist and in which truth is veiled. We rectify, love, vilify, cling, do every kind of thing based on highly ambiguous events. It's scary.

There's no vitality to the past except the life our minds give to it. The only thing the past is good for is to keep us stuck in the old patterns from which we're trying to liberate ourselves. Our personal histories are the parts of our lives which hold us where we are. What's more, the so-called "significant" parts of our personal histories bind us to patterns of behavior that become our core limitations. If we don't allow our awareness to expand beyond our past, beyond our limitations, then how do we hope to extend our horizons and our understanding into expressing anything new? How do we hope to grow?

If we think the past is the key to anything, then our horizons will forever be tied to a particular time, place, society, culture, and set of experiences, and our potential to get beyond that will be lost. We'll waste our lives judging everyone we meet and every event as a shadow of something that's finished—or should be finished. Now, that's one of my definitions of real unhappiness.

If you look to your past experience for something meaningful, the most meaningful thing you'll find is what not to do and how not to be, and you can't live from that "not" for very long. You have to practice the improvements, not the things that don't work.

Often we hope that by reaching back into the past, we'll find the information we need to heal our stresses and traumas. But all you'll find in tension is more tension. Believe me, if you insist on standing in and sifting through garbage, the only thing you're going to become is dirty at best and ill at worst.

Reliving stress does not relieve stress; obsession with trauma can only traumatize.

You cannot change your present circumstances—you cannot choose to be happy—unless you're willing to rewire the old wiring, your present nervous system, which is a product of centuries of family dynamics. Most people go about their lives based on the latent impressions of the particular family system from which they evolved. Because people are wired to be able to function within that system, they recreate their family system over and over and over again.

The seed may sprout looking slightly different from the parent plants, but eventually the seed matures to be just like the parents.

Wired a certain way, our nervous systems extend themselves to recreate the same wiring. For the most part, we're attracted to people who in some way are wired similarly to us. Again, it may look different at first, but isn't it astonishing how many times we feel locked in the same dynamic we were locked in as children with people we thought were completely different from our natal family? We find this to be true at work, in our more intimate relationships, everywhere. This is how systems are perpetuated ad infinitum. Significantly, this happens other places in nature as well: Atomic particles from the same system, when sent to different parts of the universe, tend to maintain a correspondence irrespective of the distance between them. In other words, real change doesn't happen when outward circumstances shift; change comes from hard work within.

The result of any kind of transformation should be the dissolution of the old level of wiring into a different and more effective wiring. This is one by-product of surrender, meditation practice, and the cultivation of calmness and virtue. Appropriately focused, we have the capacity to be completely rewired and freed from the serious limitations embedded in most of our family systems. But as long as we carry the same resonance, we will continue to be wired up to the old system. The idea is to change our frequency, our vibration, so that we're wired up to a higher and finer system.

By focusing on the flow, the Self, and changing our vibration, we dissolve generations of tensions, which are the residue of our latent conditioning. There's no need to be sentimental about this conditioning when we flush it. The old family system is far less personal than you might think. The world is a laboratory of energy. Whether we're discussing sub-atomic particles, solar systems, or people systems, all relationships are energetic fields where material of one kind or another is being exchanged. Layers within layers within layers of social and family structure are simply waves of energy in motion—it's not personal. It's our little self which personalizes it. How each wave of energy is perceived by us is limited by our internal wiring.

Beneath our limited wiring, there is a universal wiring, one Creative Energy, which we can access by opening our minds and cultivating a deeper part of ourselves. In this way, we begin to go from cognitive function—from thoughts, feelings, behavior—to cognitive processes—the awareness of the Creative Energy as It arises and subsides in everything. From this vantage point, we can observe the universal nature of Energy Itself, which we'll discuss in greater detail in Chapter Eight.

For now, we just need to understand that our "instincts," our "intuition," which we may prize in making major, far-reaching decisions, is probably faulty because it's a product of our conditioning and our family systems. Individual behavior simply conforms to the structure of the system in which a person is involved and may not reflect the highest potential for that person; only living from the Self does that. When we surrender, we uncover the Self, which is beyond the entanglements of the past. It's then that we have the opportunity to live from a higher and finer vibration than that of our past family systems.

So simply put: Flush everything. Do what any productive person would do with excrement—don't fondle the stuff; flush it. Every single day, flush that day; flush the years and whatever else; flush all the parts of you that you think are so significant. Your past is nothing more than former road shows put on by your little self. It's a product of all the want, desire, and brutality that you're hoping to transcend, and the way to transcend it is not to smear it all over yourself. The way to transcend it is to wish it well and send it on its way. You cut through tension, not by mucking around in it, but by reaching through it.

Ironically, though, you may create some tension at first when you let go of your personal history; as you change and grow, some of the tensions you experience will be the transcendence of attachments you've established in your pre-existing pattern. That's another way of saying that the people you know, who say they love you, often are your biggest limitations when you try to change. These people are accustomed to having their needs met in a particular way, and if you change, they don't know if they're going to get what they want. Are they going to get all the strokes they used to, or if they've been the ones caring for you, all the medals they need? It's the old "What's-going-to-happen-to-me?" symphony being played in the key of "What's-going-to-happen-to-them?" They're accustomed to orange and now it's cherry —they're upset and determined to make you feel somehow responsible. Surrender it all; if a love is real, it will just get bigger as it is surrendered and you grow.

Surrender your self with the small "s;" surrender your ego; surrender what you want, think you need, what you are doing, where you are going, what you ought to do, where you ought to be, and above all, where you have been. Surrender every part of your small self, every idea and limitation, and release a flow within you that dissolves your ego and elevates you above desire, past, present, and future. Without surrender, you have no chance to love your life and be happy because dwelling in the past, which is nothing but tension you can't resolve, will wear you down. The past is dead. Treat it that way. Bury it and move on.

There is a powerful parable in the Bible which speaks to this point. It is the story of Lot and his wife. As the couple is leaving Sodom and Gomorrah, their guiding angel tells them not to look back. But Lot's wife does look back, and she turns into a pillar of salt. This, for me, is a metaphor for what happens to anyone who starts to look back. That person becomes crystallized by the past, frozen in its patterns. It is a dead thing anyway, and because of our faulty memories, it is largely an illusion, a fabrication of our small self's needs and chemistry. It doesn't merit a second look.

The key for any of us to finding fulfillment is not to look back; it's to get the heck out of there. Why did Lot's wife look back? Was it due to sentimentality, or was it egotism, a perversity which told her she was above the rules? Whatever the motive, looking back stopped her flow in a heartbeat.

> *The answers you seek do not lie in the past; they lie precisely in the flow which is inside you now. The answers lie, as always, within you, at this moment, just as you are. The answers are not in the future, they're not in the past, they're here, now; and the moment you choose to embrace and connect to them, to your Self, and live from there, your future is transformed, your past, finished.*

The scary thing for us is that the future, when we try to look ahead, appears to be a black hole. It is that Infinite

Uncertainty we spoke of earlier. The past is less uncertain, and that's why we cling to it and find reasons to stay stuck in it. We prefer the Devil we know to the Devil we don't know. But Life just is uncertain. In order to have any chance of happiness, we have to face and embrace Uncertainty; we have to be completely at peace with and experience ourselves as totally well in the company of, in fact, in union with Infinite Uncertainty. Then life is based on what is real. Then we are at one with Life.

The only way we find that peace, that union with what is real, is to surrender. The main thing is to be at peace; that is a state of surrender. By peace, I do not mean relaxation. Surrender and relaxation are related, but they are not the same. Relaxation is the first thing you have to do before you can surrender.

Surrender also is not quite the same as letting go. It's possible to let go of a girlfriend or boyfriend, some hope for promotion, or some other such thing you want badly, and still not be a deeply surrendered person. In one moment, you may give up something specific, but such an event is finite. It's a beginning, it is one step toward surrender, but letting go, unless it becomes a way of life, is too often of a particular time and place, and, therefore, is still a function of the world of desire.

Only when you release your mind and emotions—completely surrender all the things and feelings your mind tells you are so vital—can you act in the highest best interest of everyone concerned. When you approach things from a mental perspective instead of from a state of surrender, what happens? You serve yourself, not the situation. A subtle defensiveness and self-service bleeds into the whole event; a subtle self-justification denies you the opportunity to serve the highest best interest of all.

Stop reacting to issues; act, instead, from a state of surrender in which mind and emotions are released. Liberate yourself from your defensive routines, and absorb information for the purpose of having a greater capacity to serve the interest of the whole. You are part of the whole anyway; in fact, as we will discuss in greater detail later, none of us is separate from anyone or anything in any way.

There is no "other." As a result, you will find serving the whole Self-enhancing, *not* Self-denying. Through service, we learn about real love, about how truly to love everyone and everything in our environment, and that is essential, as we already know, to the choice to be happy. As we will see later, loving the whole is tantamount to loving ourselves.

It all boils down to one simple thing: Keep your mind and your heart open and focused every day on your inner work and its expression in the world. You have to focus on your inner work and do it well—and do it with love. If you can do that, then your work is going to be, first, a little bit small and very concentrated, and then it's going to expand and expand and expand as your skill and awareness in expressing that work unfold. The main thing is, be happy; the possibilities are boundless.

Surrender is a state of being. As I said before, it is a state of peace. In that state, we see the reality of Life, we embrace its uncertainty. We see what truly nourishes and sustains us, which isn't anything the world has to offer, but something that already dwells within us. From this state, we see that our Life flows from Self, and we can attend to that flow. By cultivating where we really come from, we can find our own flowering and experience our fulfillment. No amount of striving in the world will make this happen.

To think somehow that the achievement or acquisition of something outside us is going to make us better is a foolish notion. It is just one more attempt on our parts to create the illusion of certainty where no certainty exists. Surrender transforms the void, Infinite Uncertainty, from a scary place to an experience of completeness and perfection. Instead of attempting to manipulate, twist, or deny Reality, which is Infinite Uncertainty, we simply live in conscious contact with It, and in our daily lives, we do our inner work and try to serve each and every situation in the finest way we can.

God is in all our lives, whether we're aware of it or not, God just is Life. It's our choice whether we cultivate and express the presence of God in our lives or not. To choose to be happy is to cultivate and express that

Presence, which, because it is energy and vitality, is free-flowing, unpredictable, with an intelligence and elegance of its own that does not follow our silly rules. To surrender is to be at peace with the Uncertainty that is God, to want nothing, to strive for nothing, to serve every situation. To put it simply, surrender is to flow with calmness and integrity in that unfathomable flow that is Life Itself.

The powerful experiences in our lives will either make us strong or weak, depending upon whether or not we choose to digest and grow from them. To choose Liberation, which begins with surrender, is to be liberated from personal history, from limitations, tensions, the misfortunes of the past; it is to digest everything. The past has nothing to do with anything. Even if there is no misfortune in your past, the past still has nothing to do with anything.

Surrender the past, surrender the present, surrender the future, surrender everything. Surrender to your finest, deepest Self. Forget everything except what is possible now within you.

And what is possible now within you is pure joy.

In our discussion of the past, we talked about how powerful the mind is in creating the thing we call the past. In fact, the mind is our chemistry—past, present, and future—and the only hope we have of changing our chemistry—which is the biological part of us that tells us we need this thing and that thing in order to be happy—is to quiet our minds. Notice I did not say "change our minds—the only way to change our chemistry is to change our minds"—because the mind never really changes its mode of operation. Its mode of operation is to chatter on.

But when you are able to quiet your mind, you hear what your deepest Self is saying to you. Then you act from that, which is a much truer place than you come from or get to by acting on what the mind tells you. As you progress in your inner work, as you grow, the mind still is the thing that chatters, but far below you, in the realm of the little self where you no longer live.

In the chapter on meditation, we'll talk about quieting the mind through repetition of a mantra, and we'll discuss feeling our way towards the flow rather than thinking our way towards it. But for now, simply begin by asking to be quiet and surrender. That quietness and surrender will allow you to release tensions and extend your creative energy. This is the same as saying that quieting the mind and surrendering your issues will pave the way for you to cultivate a life of calmness and virtue. Why is cultivating calmness and virtue important? Because calmness is the condition of deep internal openness which we hope will become our permanent state, and virtue is extending that openness to other people. They are two of the most important cornerstones in the choice to be happy because without them, we cannot sustain a deep connection with the Self.

Without calmness and virtue, every vision, every inspiration, any idealism that dawns within us will be reduced to a vehicle for fulfilling our limited, personal ends. Without calmness and virtue, our lives will be connected only to the small self, and that's a formula for unhappiness.

As virtuous people, we are strong in ourselves, and at the same time, we are deeply concerned with the welfare of others. The presence of virtue is necessary in order to form the deep inner vision we discussed in Chapter Two. This is because the thick and sticky chemical atmosphere existing inside a self-absorbed person denies the possibility for any authentic condensation of Creative Energy in the form of a deep inner vision. When we allow ourselves to become deeply self-absorbed, we put ourselves in a double bind: We become fearful of the world and fearful of ourselves. There's no possibility for vision and change, and we're continuously obsessed with the mantra of stupidity, "What's going to happen to me?" That is one mantra, by the way, that does not quiet the mind.

So in your choice to be happy, one of the first things you do is to quiet your mind, and from that stillness, surrender your little self to the Self and become calm and deeply open. From that state of inner calmness—which takes time to establish, both each day and over time—you move in the world with as much virtue as you can.

Some of you may be tightening at the word, "virtue," and asking what exactly I mean by it. Does it have the same connotations as Christian virtue? Virtue in this discussion is not a moral term any more than "karma" is the Hindu variant of the Christian notion of sin. Virtue here is analogous to integrity. Look up "integrity" in the dictionary; it means "the quality or state of being complete; wholeness." It comes from the same root as "integer," which means a "whole number, not a fraction," or "anything complete in itself." In addition, integrity means "the quality or state of being unimpaired; soundness" and "uprightness, honesty, sincerity."

Now doesn't this sound familiar? The core of all these definitions is precisely the quality we talked about when we discussed living from our deepest Self. Wholeness. An understanding that everything, including ourselves and our lives—no matter what our life circumstances—is wonderful just as it is; that we are whole in and of ourselves.

But I use the word "virtue" and not "integrity" in this discussion because integrity is where virtue begins. If your growth stops with you, then ultimately, it is no growth at all; it is just more stuff of the little self and can only lead to that state of self-absorbed collapse we mentioned earlier. The notion of virtue has two dimensions. Within ourselves, it is integrity—it is becoming skillful in everything we do—which requires a high degree of self-honesty and the ability to take feedback or even criticism in the proper spirit.

The second dimension of virtue is beyond the interior; it is to behave with the awareness of flow, not to create unnecessary tensions, and to speak and act toward the highest best interest of everybody involved in the situations in which we live and work. Virtue is releasing tension and allowing creative energy to flow for the benefit of everyone, not just ourselves. There is no cookbook of rules about virtue—no one way to do things. Virtue is not a moral issue; it is about values instead. Morals are imposed on you by other people and by social convention. Values evolve from within you. Morals are behavioral by design; values are substantive. Being chaste or some such moral behavior is not being virtuous. Virtuous is being "good," yes, but not in the Christian sense; virtue is goodness because virtue is releasing tension, within oneself and in one's environment. Virtue is having the capacity to go anywhere, experience anything, and maintain your integrity at all times.

Virtue is the ability to walk through hell without getting the hair on your feet singed.

Practicing virtue means that you will always keep your values in front of you because, among other things, they will enliven your deep inner vision of your Self and your Life. Having a higher and finer vision of your Self and where you want to live on the pendulum is not enough; you must express the values of that vision in the world as well. This is why it's important to remember exactly what your values are every minute of every day.

You cannot allow your work in the world to precede your values. Often, we see a kind of expediency manifest in people who, because they have no values, fall into lust, greed, selfishness, confusion, arrogance, egotism—all the antitheses of virtue.

People fall into these behaviors by thinking: "I'm in thus-and-such a business, and it requires me to do this and that. As a result, I will mistreat my friends and behave not-so-virtuously, but that's only temporary. When I'm done with my business, I'll have money and be able to be a calm and virtuous person, and then I'll be really nice to everyone and everything. I'll be calm and virtuous once I have enough money."

Wrong. You have to be calm and virtuous now. Without that, there is no chance for you to choose to be happy. There is always a better way to do something and a better time to do it, and the time is now and the way is clear. In moving through life, recognize how you can think and behave in such a manner that continually speaks to and expresses that better way. That's being virtuous.

Virtue is a mechanism by which we come to understand ourselves more deeply and extend our awareness through our experiential life. We must be strong inside ourselves first before we can display virtue, but once we've made that deep connection with the Self and are living from that, we have found value inside ourselves; in order for that value to grow, we will eventually have to, and naturally want to, share it with others. In this way, we create and reinforce sources of nourishment which, over time, uplift us and those around us. Practicing virtue, we continuously revitalize our connections as we create within ourselves the bridge toward an ever more refined quality of contact with people and life.

In our lives, either there is something we want to do or something we want to be; this must be a clear distinction for each of us because if there's something we want to do more than something we want to be, then the doing will structure our lives. For example, let's say we want to be world-famous jazz musicians. That will require that we move to New York or whichever jazz center we desire and spend lots of time schmoozing and so forth, and while that may not be a bad thing, it will take a lot of energy, and we may lose the means to become the kind of people we envision ourselves as capable of being. Realizing our highest potential is a very different activity from realizing career goals. In the former, we're talking about cultivating calmness and virtue; in the latter, contacts with the people who launch careers. The music business, whatever business, is largely politics. That's why I am a spiritual teacher and not a proponent of the religion business.

When we are concerned with *being* something, we make different choices. We still make compromises, but of a different kind. They will be the compromises we have to make to serve the highest best interest of a situation, not just our own self-interest. This is the distinction between a vision of what we might do, which is a lower vision, and the vision of who we might be. To see ourselves in terms of the quality of our person, in terms of depth, clarity, discrimination, capacity for giving or self-sacrifice, in other words, in terms of calmness and virtue, is quite different. I won't be any more specific than that because, once again, there is no cookbook for what "being" will look like in you.

But it is important to understand that when we emphasize being, we are not talking about not doing; we're talking about our priorities and values. When we place our values first and recognize that our doing is a mechanism through which those values flow, then, to return to our example, it's possible for us to move to New York and be concerned with who we are rather than where we must get to. We might endeavor seriously to become virtuous people and to manifest that virtue in the field of music. Because we are concerned with virtue and refuse to take time away from doing our inner work and because we refuse to conduct ourselves in certain ways to get ahead, perhaps we'll be denied the opportunity to make it to the top, perhaps not. There may be a compromise we have to make. But we will have made it and retained our integrity; we will have retained our deep connection with the Self. We will, once again, have made the choice to be happy instead of dwelling in the world of short-term gains and long-term decay.

If our focus is growing, then we can do, do, do and not lose our perspective on being. But we need to make sure we're not kidding ourselves about the quality of our growth while we're busy doing.

Thinking about what we want to do and focusing on doing it is better than thinking about our so-called problems. Shifting our attention from our noodles to *doing* something more with our lives is a step forward. But the issue is, how far are we going to step? We can take one step forward and *do* something we want to do, or we can take a few more steps and *be* the finest people we can be, growing people—even spiritually growing people. In that case, we won't be concerned about what we want to do anymore. Rather, we will be concerned about what is possible. We will begin to understand the creative process and our own inner resources in an energetic sense—not intellectually. Then, it will be a new and wonderful life for us.

A person who values inner work has the vision of a deep connection with the Self and maintains a spiritual practice in order to sustain that connection. Such a person chooses contemplation over other things. This does *not* mean that we live a life without work or relationships in the world. We spend our committed time each day in meditation and still live a relatively busy life. But when our values are calmness and virtue, we cultivate those values within ourselves first and foremost every day. Then we go into the world to express those values, to test our understanding of them, and to have that understanding tested. This is life in its many facets.

We want to create within ourselves a capacity for Self-dependency, recognizing that only that platform allows us authentically to participate in a life of inner work. Only when we are Self-dependent do we have the choice of whether to do or to be—to choose our own values. Otherwise, our values are something superimposed on us, and that is not real growth.

Having arrived at that level of Self-dependency, we each decide the issues of doing and being. We choose our own values and, having chosen, either strive to acquire what we want or strive to become the kind of person we want to be. In either case, there is powerful potential for us to learn many lessons and to continue to grow.

Ultimately, if we are considerate, choosing to get or to do something will kick us back into recognizing the importance of who we are as human beings, especially when dealing with people who lack integrity and whose only value is survival. Like a douse of cold water in the face, contact with the world of doing and getting will return us to what we want to be and to our focus on spiritual growth.

Virtue serves humanity, and the point of our virtue is our concern with human suffering, which arises because we experience it ourselves. Isn't that what brings us to a spiritual practice? We experience suffering and say, "I can't live like this anymore. There has to be a different way."

Reaching this point, we find that there is something we can do about suffering: We can choose to be filled with a sense of well-being by doing our inner work, and we can extend that sense of well-being to those around us so that our presence in their lives will be of some benefit to them instead of a source of tension for them and for us.

What is suffering really but tension? And so alleviating suffering, someone else's or our own, is the same as releasing tension and allowing creative energy to flow, which is the same as growing. When we dedicate our lives to calmness and virtue, we are dedicating our lives, once again, to growth. Calmness and virtue mature into compassion and consideration; none of these qualities is ideologically based; they simply manifest in the lives of those around us by our calm and virtuous presence.

You must become strong and calm inside yourself first before you extend your compassion to others. Otherwise, you may be giving energy you need for your own growth. Often, people don't realize the degree to which authentic self-discipline and true responsibility are involved when we give of ourselves. Sometimes, too, what some people call being "open and in the flow" becomes a strategy for avoiding conflict or for repressing responsibility for some unfortunate situation.

To focus on calmness and virtue, you must be centered. This means you begin to relate to and take responsibility for whatever tensions exist within you and your environment. Talking about openness and flow can be a way of sandstorming a discussion. Such talk can kick up every kind of issue except the real one at hand. You must think about what it is you do to aggravate a situation, take responsibility for that aggravation, and contemplate how to resolve any tension in the highest best interest of everyone concerned, including yourself.

People who talk openness and flow without authentically experiencing that state alienate themselves from their environment. These talkers think they're flowing and open while causing everyone around them extreme frustration from the tension created by their flowier-than-thou attitude. Talking flow doesn't create flow. At these times, cultivate your own calmness and virtue, do your own work, and develop the discrimination to know with whom you can share your life and with whom you can't.

You may be thinking, "I see the wisdom of what is being said, I want to live a life of unconditional love, of calmness and virtue; I want to choose to be happy; I'm going to meditate every day; but—all this sounds like a tall order on my own."

You're right. To say to yourself, "I will live a life of unconditional love" and then to go out there and face the abusers, the brutality, or even less dramatically, we hope, something as inescapable as your own boss, spouse, or children—to say this and try to do it alone, without an environment or person to guide and support you in any way, is difficult indeed if not impossible. You would be drained in a flash and quite angry that your best efforts at living life from a deeper place kept ending only in deep frustration.

You have to have a fundamental point of reference, a place to begin, a place to focus. If you're going to have the highest achievement that is available to a human being in this life, there still has to be a first place to put your foot down, a point of departure, and a place to which you can continually refer, which is at once accessible and at the same time in no way limited.

And that place, that first step, the point of departure, is a very simple one—it is the teacher. Before you can learn to meditate, you must be taught, and before you can express the finest person you are, someone must mirror fineness for you. A teacher continually gives you feedback on your own state by their mere company. A teacher also points out the potential for you to be in a deeper state and serves as a model for observing how one person, at least, acts out an undifferentiated awareness in a very differentiated environment.

It's like fly-fishing; you can learn more from watching a really good caster for about an hour than you can from reading all the books and looking at all the videos on fly-casting. Watch a great fly-caster, observe the rhythm of the movements, see what is done, subtle and gross. This is how you learn. Then try it yourself: Stick a few flies in the back of your head, bean yourself a couple of times, choke yourself with a weighted line, and realize it's not as easy as it looks. Practice more.

A spiritual teacher is like the expert fly-caster: You watch that person work, and while you may not know exactly what you're about, you recognize something good when you see it in them, and so the teacher provides you with a certain level of clarity. Clarity comes from looking deep within yourself and continuing to look deeper until you begin to have that vision of what you really want your life to be; then you look at the teacher and see your vision in action.

The teacher helps you compress the field of your vision, to focus your vision. To experience a vision of what you really want, you have to focus deeply within yourself for as long as it takes. The teacher teaches you the discipline, the practice, necessary to do that. While concentrating on your internal vision, you have an external vision—this is your experience of connection with the teacher, a person who has not only chosen to live, but actually does live, every single second of every single day in that state of deep surrender, of deep well-being, that you, yourself, are trying to achieve through your choice to be happy.

THE TEACHER

*T*HERE ARE LOTS of books
on the subject of being your own spiritual teacher. Such
books make me chuckle because saying you can be your
own spiritual teacher is like saying you can teach yourself
dentistry or neurosurgery. Spirituality is similar; it's something we have the potential to do, but it requires guidance
and skill. After all, if contact with the Self, with that deep
sense of well-being, were so easy to establish, this world
would be a very different place.

To have contact with a living person who is established in the experience of Spirit is to go beyond our
individual suffering to live from the Self.

I've been asked many times whether it's possible to have
a teacher who is no longer living. Such a person certainly
can inspire us. But spiritual work is about transformation,

and this transformation is only possible with a living teacher who is both established in Spirit and here for us now. That's because a living teacher is an energy field, an energy source. When the student first comes to the teacher, that student is like ice. Ice is not a bad thing; ice is fine. It is perfectly cold and perfectly solid. However, its capacity for nourishing anything is limited. To nourish anything, it must become water. The transition from ice to water requires heat; the heat absorbed into the ice brings about the transformation in the ice, which is called a change of state.

If the finer qualities within us are to emerge and nourish our Life, it is necessary that an energy source be applied to us as well. Otherwise, our finer qualities are always functioning through the crystal ice block of our tensions and trauma, the limitations we accumulate as we move through the world. A teacher, then, is a source from which we draw energy, heat, which allows for a transformation to take place.

A teacher is also a subtle constraint, and for the constraint to work, the teacher must be a physical presence in our lives. As a change of state occurs, the energy cannot become diffuse or the change will not take place. The constraint that is the teacher discourages diffusion of energy. It takes as much energy for ice to go from 32 degrees to 33 degrees, in other words, to melting, as it does for it to go from zero to 32. The last degree requires as much energy as all the energy that went into bringing the ice to the point where the shift can happen. Spiritual work is similar. A student can work very hard for a time and then decide that he or she just can't work anymore, and that student can be one degree from the change he or she is seeking. The teacher knows this; the teacher cannot do the work for the student, but the teacher can quietly encourage the student not to dissipate his or her energy at such a critical time.

The teacher is never a big constraint; a teacher doesn't have a thumb on a student ever, but because of the connection, because you care about that connection and the working together, the teacher functions as a kind of definition, a structure within your life which supports the work you're trying to do. Further, the subtle constraint that is the teacher also brings out from within you your capacity for respect, first for the teacher and then for all human beings, all living things, for Life Itself. Without respect, a person comes only from his or her own selfish awareness, which is a severe limitation.

Our need for a teacher is based on our need for someone who can help us get beyond limitation, who understands our deepest potential better than we do. An authentic teacher will help us deal with our egotism by shedding light on everything we say and do, everything we think we are. That light will illuminate the truth for us when we have lost it. This is why we act with devotion to the teacher—we want to operate on behalf of our highest Self, and the teacher relates only from that Self to that Self. Demonstrating respect for a teacher, therefore, demonstrates respect for our Self.

Devotion to the teacher is really devotion to our own work; it shows our commitment to unconditional love as a means of annihilating our personal suffering and all human suffering because the event that is the teacher has at its core nothing but real love. The authentic teacher is constantly working every sinew, fibre, and blood vessel in himself or herself for the benefit of the student. That is the only way real transformation takes place. The teacher is willing to be both a human generator of energy, of love, and a human garbage disposal of tension. Both functions take an unimaginable toll.

The love of a teacher is of a magnitude unfathomable by most people, and this is one reason why authentic spiritual teachers are venerated in their cultures—because there is a recognition that they are living examples of states that transcend anything around which we can wrap our minds. They are living examples of pure love.

Sacrifice is the essence of selfless service. Service as I speak of it is not drudgery but a source of joy. The love manifest in service drives away fear. When your heart is full of real love, you don't even notice the things that scare you. Love, openness, are always the antidotes to tension, and what is fear but tension?

In order for our lives to change, we have to be open to change, and the devotion we display in the presence of a teacher facilitates our ability to change. True devotion enables us to take feedback and change in a flash. Limited devotion leaves us justifying our current position. If you want your life to be different, then it has to change, and you have to change, and the fulcrum point in the discussion is the respect and devotion you have for the teacher as someone who will help you see the changes you need to make and help you make them.

The love and devotion we display toward a teacher is a crucial part of the transformation process because it is the love and devotion that ultimately transforms us. The books on spiritual practice say you need a teacher, and they say you have to be loving and devoted to that teacher. But it is important that you understand this: The point is not the teacher; the point is the love and devotion. The teacher does not need your love and devotion. She is already a master of herself; he is already calm and virtuous, surrendered, deeply open, loving life, happily living from the Self. You need to practice love and devotion—that is the kind of person you need to be in order to have that deep sense of well-being and fulfillment that your teacher already has. It's as simple as that.

Devotion is a powerful and important practice. It isn't saccharine; it is work; and it begins with surrendering yourself to God's will, to the highest Energy, to Life Itself, and ends in no particular time and place, in no particular form. It's the quality of your devotion that opens up a special place within you and allows for a special kind of connection to exist, a connection that transforms your life from the inside out.

I've had wonderful, dynamic, incredibly free, loving, and confusing teachers. I've had disciplined, serious, hard, apparently uncaring, impossible-to-relate-to teachers; I've had people I learned a lot from who were not teachers per se. But I was filled with love and devotion throughout all these experiences; I continually kept my heart open, and that smashed all the idols. That love penetrated through all the forms into the holistic, unified, undifferentiated, infinite, loving essence of Life Itself. And that is what our work with a teacher does.

It's not that you're devoted to some other person in your devotion to a teacher. If God is not "other" than you, how can the teacher be? In your devotion to an authentic spiritual teacher, you're devoted to your own deepest potentiality, the power of Life within you. You are not devoted to a person, you are devoted to the Self, which is in you and in everyone. Devotion and respect are vehicles for continuously transcending the small self. If you can practice genuine respect with a teacher, you can practice respect with anybody, and if you can't practice it with a teacher, then you'll never practice it at all.

Another way to talk about devotion is surrender— again, not surrender to the teacher, but surrender to the deepest part of you. Surrender is the mechanism by which the rate in a flow increases, and in the presence of a teacher, surrender is analogous to a fine vapor of steam being created from water when it is heated up. Movement in the earth's atmosphere occurs because energy moves constantly from high to low pressure in order to distribute itself, and as with weather, the teacher is a higher pressure source moving to distribute its energy in a lower pressure environment, which is this world and us. To the degree we are able to surrender, a flow takes place with the help of the teacher, and this flow establishes the potential for spontaneous changes within us.

Put a pan of water over a fire, and the fire's energy becomes absorbed into both the water and the metal of the pan. As energy is absorbed, the water changes state. Like the element that is water, we, too, are a collection of molecules in a state of disequilibrium, and that disequilibrium not only makes change possible, but certain. As a result, we don't have to accept our notions about our limitations; we don't have to remain ice, we don't even have to remain water.

"But," you might say, "why not remain water? Water nourishes every living thing."

This is true; water causes growing things to flourish, and on a certain level—the level of just keeping things alive —such nourishment is noble and completely necessary.

But steam runs engines; steam is power, with many different potentials to it. If you think only of the miraculous properties of water in its liquid state, then you will not understand what can be done with the subtler states of water, like steam. You're limited by your mind telling you that water is a good thing—it was good for your forefathers, it's been good for you, and so on. And it *is* a good thing; it is wonderful and completely necessary for nourishment.

But there are finer states of being, more powerful and productive states, available to the molecules which make up water. Likewise, if you're not bound by the body, which tells you that water is the only ticket, then you can see the possibility of far more powerful and productive states available to you than the one you're currently in or the one you're going to be in next week, next month, or next year—or the one you *want* to be in.

Surrendering and allowing your true nature to emerge in the company of a teacher increases the rate of flow and the amount of energy you are able to absorb. This increased flow creates the possibility of a change of state, which is what you seek if you're determined to be a growing person. But the idea is not to focus on any *thing* the teacher can do for you; in other words, if you're just devoted because you want the teacher to wave a magic wand and make you into a powerful steam-genie, you're missing the point. Connection with the teacher is not about acquiring some benefit which is absent or lost; it's about your connection with the Self deep within you. Everything you need to grow is right here, right now— the teacher facilitates that growth, but he or she does not *give* it to you. Intrinsic to ice is the possibility of the state known as water; intrinsic to water is the state known as steam; fire is the catalyst.

The connection with the teacher helps us recognize that deepest Creative Energy which is inside us, but to which we've forgotten the possible pathways. The teacher lights the way. The teacher helps us find the stillpoint at the top of the pendulum, the stillpoint of the Self, where the teacher already lives.

Without commitment to the Self and to a spiritual practice, and without trust in a teacher, we won't get far on the pathway to happiness and fulfillment. Commitment—and remember, it is commitment to our Self, not to any "other" or any thing outside of us—is deciding what we really want to do and then doing it; trust is allowing the power of love inside us to expand and transform our mind, emotions, and physical life. If we remain the same old guarded selves, easily unnerved by any strong experience, then what can we hope to achieve?

Every great person I've known has busted my ass. Such a notion may concern some of you: How can a teacher's love and nourishment bust anybody's ass? If the teacher and Self are the same, why would there be any need to bust ass? At different times, the face of love looks different, depending upon what is required to inspire a student to higher heights. An authentic teacher demands what seems to be the impossible from a student in order to show that student the great things the student already has within her Self.

Every teacher has forced me—because it's what I wanted to be demanded from me—every teacher has demanded from me deep work, great things, and that has been a true blessing. That is why the highest benefit a teacher can give a student is to destroy that student.

Does this seem shocking? Think about it for a minute in light of what we've said about the small self. When I say, "destroyed," I don't mean to scare you. Be scared, if you must, it's a real thing, but all a teacher is going to destroy in you is what we said must be destroyed in order for you to grow—your misunderstanding. The only thing you must give up to the heat of the energy field that is your teacher is your misunderstanding, your limitations, your crystallization. This is how your ice becomes water and your water, something as refined and powerful as steam, which is the potential of the Creative Energy in you.

We grow up trying to protect ourselves from having our hearts broken and our feelings hurt. A teacher is not interested in building a shell around our hearts for protection. A teacher encourages us to get our hearts open, now, this minute, to break our hearts, if we must, in order to get them open, to experience a flow.

Break your heart, have it broken by the recognition of the limited existence, the ice, that most human beings settle for in the face of the extraordinary potential that exists within.

To realize the unlimited potential that is Spirit Itself, Life Itself, is to be destroyed because this recognition puts an end to our smallness, our sense that we are a separate, little person with important, separate, little concerns which must be attended to. This separateness—this grave misunderstanding—is the cause of alienation, frustration, doubt, fear, suffering in all our lives. To have a teacher is to put us in touch with a place beyond an individual life; we are destroyed, but in a wonderful way.

To have an authentic teacher is to be released from the limitations of time and place. There is no way to wrap your mind around the event that is the teacher. If you have a chance to have some power in your life which nourishes and uplifts you, even if it breaks your brain, accept it. Embrace it. If it breaks your heart, let it, and love it more. It's a way you can become free of your little self, free of your material issues, of trauma and strain.

The teacher isn't necessarily going to fit into your idea of what a teacher ought to look like or be like. Rudi wasn't the first person I met who said he was a spiritual teacher, but he was the only one who was authentic. He was real. The rest of them were nice, very sweet, very holy-looking, and somewhat shallow. I met lots of those.

Rudi looked me in the eye and broke my heart into a thousand pieces. Fortunately, I knew what I was looking at, and I valued it from the beginning. But it was in the most unlikely setting—Manhattan, the transition zone between the East and West Village. Everything about it was unlikely: Rudi ate hot dogs, conducted business; he was an Oriental art dealer and a great one. But in spite of these incongruities, the entire event had a substance to it which was palpable, a boundless power and sweetness.

There was so much magic scintillating around Rudi. I remember once he gave a talk, during which some people hassled him about the donuts in an ashram bakery; the donuts had sugar in them. These people wanted to know why the sweetener wasn't honey, or something they considered to be purer than cane sugar. So Rudi explained that some people eat pure food and turn it into poison, but a spiritual person eats poison and turns it into love.

That is the essence of what a spiritual teacher does— he or she takes in every kind of poisonous tension and turns it into nourishment for the deepest part of us.

The goal of inner work is Liberation, and from what are we liberated? Suffering, which is tension. As long as an individual sees himself as separate in the world, struggling with other individuals for limited resources, suffering is inevitable. The teacher makes it possible for us to have the courage to put an end to this notion of separateness by nourishing our contact with the big Self while encouraging constraint of the small self's agenda.

The teacher is a physical demonstration of the Truth that: There is no other.

A teacher encourages us to open our hearts and let whatever happens happen. He or she is someone who cares enough to try to evoke from within us the finest that is there. The teacher is not someone who gives us an ideology; one ideology is as good as another because no manmade ideology is big enough to hold the Truth. The real gift of an authentic spiritual teacher is to release the Vital Force in us from the limitations, the tensions, which have existed in us for generations.

Our connection with the energy field that is the teacher is a sacred space because that point of contact is where we begin to experience the subtle fluctuation of essential Creative Energy, which is God.

Open to and cultivate that contact, open to it more and more, and increasingly you'll find the subtle creative power which is alive within you, which can transform your life to the degree that you allow at any given moment. Slowly, this contact with a living teacher brings you into total awareness of the Infinite Teacher, the Self, which is the essence of all of Life. It is that Teacher to which we are all connected. But it is only by contact with and due to the love of living teachers that we have the energy to overcome our own patterns of limitation, our fears and resistances, in order to become established in the awareness of that Infinite Teacher.

To put it simply, the teacher—and devotion to the teacher—frees us from the fundamental constriction known as "me"; only when we transcend what is "me"-driven do we have the possibility to be free of desire. One purpose of having a teacher is to stop us from thinking about ourselves—even for five minutes. To become devoted to the highest and finest part of us—which is manifest in the teacher and in our contact with the teacher—is to release ourselves, to extend ourselves, to connect to and then to reabsorb that vibration, that energy, that power which is the essence of Life Itself.

When we surrender to the Self, we merge with the divine and rise beyond our individual limited selves to become what we truly are—at one with the Energy, the flow and source of our lives and of all Life. We understand then that every thing is one thing because every thing is simply a manifestation of divine Energy.

Doing our inner work is the same as worship—it is surrendering our little selves to a higher force that is in contact with the fundamental ground of experience itself, of Life Itself. But—and this is very important—any worship which places the teacher above us is absolutely not true worship. If anything, such a practice is dualistic and perpetuates misunderstanding because it doesn't recognize the fundamental Truth: an authentic teacher and the Self are one. As we've said before, it is all one thing, differentiated manifestations, yes, but the same Energy. The teacher is not above you.

Because the teacher is not above you, if he or she is authentic, he won't make up rules, she won't give out grades, the teacher will not tell you what to do or to be. He or she will help you uncover your potentialities, but what you do with them is up to you. An authentic teacher wishes for *you* to discover what your life will be. Within every person, there is a creative power that has its own program, and it's not up to the teacher to decide what that program will be. The teacher does not work on anybody; he or she simply participates in the creative flow and understands that reaching through the tensions will expand that flow and allow for a state of total well-being to manifest. From that state, your Life will express the perfection that it is.

The teacher absolutely is not in your life to work on your problems. He or she cannot work on your problems because the deepest part of you, which is all the teacher cares about and is in contact with, has no problems. As a teacher, I'm not interested in the slightest about what anyone thinks is wrong with them. I know that there is something in everyone which is profoundly right, and that's the only place in my students to which I wish to relate. If you stay in contact with that place in yourself and respond honestly and directly based on that understanding, then whatever vibration you come in contact with in the presence of your teacher will change into the vibration which is the experience of Truth.

An authentic teacher wishes only for you to be Self-dependent, to choose your own values, to have the choice of "to do" or "to be," or of how to interweave both into your life. The real test of any teaching is the degree to which it creates people who are Self-dependent. With my students, I try to foster Self-dependence, not dependence on me or on a community. I could create a monastic situation in which people would become dependent on me. That would be a solid basis for the religion business. But it's not the way to share an authentic Life.

Ultimately, we must be Self-dependent and have the ability to think and talk intelligently, to take feedback with a minimum of moaning and groaning, to make decisions about our own lives. Having this capacity, we can change and grow and be of value to ourselves and those people whose lives our life touches. This paves the way for an authentic, dynamic interaction on a higher level with our teacher and everyone around us. In addition, if we cultivate calmness and virtue, which are at the core of Self-dependence, we can sustain an even stronger contact and connection. This creates the opportunity to experience a merging which transcends human suffering. Thus, Self-dependence, far from encouraging any kind of separateness from the teacher, pushes us toward the experience of oneness with the Creative Energy to which the teacher is the doorway.

Surrender allows us to sustain an experience of complete connection with the teacher, but at such a moment of connection, we're not merging with the teacher as a personality. At such a moment, it is our own Universal Soul with which we rediscover oneness. We extend ourselves to encompass something beyond our biological identity, and this reveals our true nature to us—a nature which is definitely not what we thought it was because it is not of the world of decay and desire, of biology. It is one with the Creative Energy that is the Source of all Life.

Intrinsic to that release of the world of desire and self and the experience of merging with the Soul is a loving joy. It is the essence of our inner work with a teacher. I still take time every day to remember my teachers and to bow within myself to them. I am truly grateful because I understand what my life would have been without them. I am intensely grateful for the choices I have, which they revealed to me. I recognize that, in the big picture, the suffering, pain, and disappointment I experience on occasion operates to my benefit, and I realize this only because of the understanding imparted to me by my teachers.

At the beginning of this chapter, we said that you cannot be your own teacher. But we also reaffirmed that if you truly want to grow, you can—and even must—do inner work and do it well. A master of meditation is not some being exalted above you. Such a person becomes a master through hard work, through repetition over and over again of the skills necessary to do the job. Mastery of some of the most extraordinary things has to do with just being willing to do the dumb, boring stuff over and over again and to like it while you're doing it. That's how anyone becomes great at anything.

Say you're an athlete, a tennis player, a basketball player. You practice until there's nothing to think about; there's just a flow of energy. And you practice time and time again to a degree that the feeling for what you're doing is so strong, you don't have to look at the basket to put the ball in—you can do all kinds of things ordinary people can't because you've done it so often and with such attention that you *feel* it, you feel every nuance in every movement.

The same is true of your inner work. The only way you learn is by repetition. You practice because it's only then that the real esoteric understanding of anything—the inside knowledge of anything—becomes available. The teacher reminds you of this over and over again, a million times if necessary, a million and one times, if that's what it takes for you to get it, and it's wonderful when someone cares enough to do this with you.

Eastern philosophical texts, both Buddhist and Hindu, bring up the issue of disgust with the world. It's easy to see why—the older we get, the more disgusting the world can seem. The smoke and dust of a brutal world turn out to be a disappointment, and we seem to be wasting our time in any effort we make, and our time isn't very long in the first place. The pressure of life and the discomfort and confrontation with it are so ugly, they cause people either to get real or to quit living. Most people choose to quit living and shut down.

But by associating with an authentic spiritual teacher, we see a way to live in the world and to express ourselves as individuals that is not in conflict with other individuals and is always manifesting as value for and service to the highest best interest of the whole. This is very different from a support group—we're not giving and taking support. Instead we're identifying with that place in which each person's highest best interest merges, and then we live from and work in that place. This is spiritual mastery, the unity of Spirit and the world. In that state, disgust and disappointment—everything but deep well-being and happiness—disappear.

There is no one spiritual path; and so when you live in the presence of someone who has lived in the presence of someone who has lived in the presence of someone, you can absorb into yourself the flavor of that state of profound happiness and love that is the teacher. Sometimes, when we're forced by life to look at ourselves in a new way, we're not pleased with what we see; and it's magical to have someone to look at who reminds us of, in fact resonates, a quality of unconditional love that allows us to rise above the strain and trauma of the world in order to live in a simple, totally well place all the time, no matter what. No doctrine or dogma is necessary, no particular structure—just us in contact with Us through the living field of energy that is the Teacher.

In spiritual communities throughout the world, there's lots of talk about this spiritual master and that spiritual master and whether this one's better than that one and so forth and so on. But let me tell you the truth about the greatest living spiritual master: That master lives in you. Lives in you. In you. In you. Not anywhere else. Lives in you. You may need a little practice finding that master and then cultivating contact with that master, but the master lives in you.

Why is that? Because there is no duality between teacher and Self: All human beings derive their essence from the same source. It is all one thing. There is no other. That is why surrender is always to God; love and devotion, to God; commitment, to God. Deepest part of you, Self, God, Love, Vital Force, Flow, teacher, Teacher, Energy. It is all one thing. It is of God.

Do you want to see the greatest living spiritual master? I encourage it. Practice, do your inner work, learn from your teacher. Practice.

Learn for yourself that the greatest living spiritual master lives in the heart of you.

6

CHAPTER

INNER WORK

Spiritual Discipline and
a Guided Meditation

*P*EOPLE COME TO a spiritual
practice because they recognize the discrepancy between
what they are and what their potential is. They say,
"People think I'm this, but that's not what's in my heart.
I don't want to be 'this.' I know there's something more
inside me. How do I get to it?"

For me, spiritual practice is the answer, and this begins
with a regular meditation practice. But my particular
spiritual practice is not a verbal exercise, and once I've
instructed a student in the basic concepts and techniques
of breathing, of releasing tension, of mantra and chakras,
of opening the heart, of surrender, and finally of meditation itself, the student must learn for himself or herself
how all of it actually works. This is done through individual practice, personal commitment, by reflecting on the

experience. In other words, the student has to do her or his own spiritual work and pay attention at the same time, which is the only way to understand.

It's the student's responsibility to make a practice work. When we're first inclined in this direction, our initial experience, which is usually productive, will last for some time. Perhaps for a year or even a couple of years, powerful changes will occur in us. This will seem amazing and not too difficult. However, this initial set of changes has everything to do with the teacher and little to do with us. It has to do with the teacher's energy, with divine grace, with the effect of having layers of tension peeled away. The experience is dazzling. But our effort isn't creating the transformation at this point; it's the teacher's energy that's doing the transforming. Subsequent to these easy, superficial changes, a period comes when things seem harder; fewer easy changes remain.

Now we learn something about ourselves: We learn whether or not we're really committed to growing and to the practice which will allow change to take place within us. Change will come, but it will probably not look like what we had in mind—it will be what God wants for us, which may not be what we had in mind. Were we to get what we had in mind, we would get something limited by our state at the moment, which we're saying we wish to change. If we always got what *we* wanted, we would never realize our true potential.

The coalescing of Creative Energy takes any form It desires; it has nothing to do with what we want. Each of us gets the vision that is truly possible, which represents a transcendent level of awareness and creative expression. If we are deeply surrendered, whatever the change, it's just the change we've been looking for.

As a person starts to release all his accumulated hurt and dysfunction, it's possible to become a bit cranky. The various meditation exercises, and the constraints we put on the outward movement of our individual energy, heat us up inside, changing our frequency—mentally and emotionally as well as biochemically. When our bodies heat up just a little bit, our muscle chemistry changes.

From the change in muscle chemistry, our mental and emotional chemistry changes. This changes our understanding, and all of this is why inner work is work—it can hurt sometimes. Growing can hurt. As we detoxify, we may not always feel absolutely fabulous, but we find this is okay. It passes and the rewards are worth it; well-being becomes our permanent state over time; anxiety decreases dramatically and eventually disappears. In fact, this is where inner work becomes exciting because if a person sticks to it, it works, and this period when many people give up because it feels too much like work is precisely the time when the most beneficial changes are about to take place.

Rudi called inner work, a work of work. We have to do it for ourselves; we have to sit down every single day, preferably twice a day, relaxing and opening, circulating our attention around the inner flow of energy and breath, settling and dissolving our minds into the deepest part of our being. This is what brings about total transformation.

In your choice to be happy, in living beyond anxiety, the central equation is one Rudi emphasized again and again: Depth over time. Practice deeply every day and over time; you and your life will be transformed. Work with love, with as much joy as you can muster at any given moment; work with passion and intensity. This will transform the repetition of the event into an extraordinary occurrence full of magic.

What you are mastering in a spiritual practice is your small self; you are making it very real that you can be happy simply because you choose to be—because you are willing to do the work to be happy. Through your practice, you become a master of the self in service to the Self.

You do your inner work to contact the Self; you do not do it for anybody else. You definitely do not do this work for your teacher. The teacher is like the pool where you go to swim; it is a universal pool where you have to take the first step and dive in for yourself. If you don't know how to swim, you learn; and you don't think about how much water you're going to swallow in the process.

The first thing you do in your meditation practice is to quiet the mind because the mind is constantly worried

CHOOSE TO BE HAPPY

about how much water will be swallowed. There's a Frank Zappa song I like. In it, Zappa asks, "What's the ugliest part of your body? What's the ugliest part of your body?" Then he goes on, "Some say, your nose; others think, your toes." He concludes, "I say it's your mind."

The mind is powerful because its thoughts determine your emotions, which in turn determine your chemistry. You cannot connect to the deepest part of you, where everything is already well and happy, if your mind is full of doubts and fears. In other words, you cannot surrender, which is the key to inner work, without quieting the mind first. So, the mind is only "ugly" if you let it be.

In most meditation practices, the teacher instructs the student to repeat a mantra—a sound or phrase of sounds which may also be words—over and over again as the student meditates. The idea behind mantra repetition is to protect the mind. At first, a student repeats a mantra, which literally means "protector of the mind," in order to shift his or her attention away from unproductive thoughts. This is the lowest form of the use of mantra.

The mantra is usually repeated by the student to himself silently, without uttering a sound. When the student repeats the mantra, she is not at war with her mind; through meditation, a student is refining the mind, bringing its energy to a much higher level than that toward which it would normally gravitate.

Each mantra, and there are many different ones, has a vibration to it, and the vibration of the mantra is considered to be the same as the energy, the vitality, the presence of God. Over time, the vibration of a mantra resonates through the entire nervous system, changing the old chemistry, which was based on doubts and fears generated by old thought processes. At this point in a meditation practice, the mantra is no longer in the mind because the repetition has quieted the mind; there are no longer even syllables left to the sound of the mantra. There is simply a vibration in the nerves and in the breath that is silently transforming an individual's awareness and understanding. This is the highest level of mantra practice.

When the teacher gives a student a mantra, it's really a piece of the teacher; it is the vibration of Vital Force manifesting in the teacher and then re-manifesting grossly as sound. The student repeats that mantra over and over until it resonates deeply inside, changing individual chemistry completely. It is that change in chemistry which allows the student to live beyond his anxieties.

The mantra I give my students in the beginning is one Rudi gave me, and it is simple but powerful: "I wish to grow." As they meditate, my students may repeat over and over to themselves at each sitting, which is usually about forty-five minutes long, "I wish to grow, I wish to grow, I wish to grow." A variant of this mantra is: "I wish to surrender and grow."

But no growth is possible, no matter how fervently a person asks, if he meditates by thinking his way rather than feeling it. By the word, "feeling," I don't mean anything saccharine; "love" and "feeling" in spiritual practice are not saccharine entities. "Feeling" simply means the opposite of thought; "feeling your way" means reaching deeply into yourself and knowing, understanding, embracing the Truth you find there. The point is that true spirituality is not a belief system. It is not something in your head. The flow doesn't solve problems, and it isn't there to make you into anything the commercial world says is wonderful. Meditation is not the time to sit and think, "How do I get this or that? Who said what to whom? Where does she get off doing that to me?" And so on.

Meditation isn't the time to think anything. It's the time to check your baggage at the door. Gather yourself together, leave aside your tensions, repeat your mantra from as deep a place as you can, and start to resonate something finer and deeper within you. Reach inside and feel, connect; increasingly relax your body and mind so that the tensions and the patterns of your physical chemistry do not obstruct the expansion and, ultimately, the expression of your Self.

Maybe doing this isn't always possible, maybe this thing and that thing just are distracting you, but try. You have your work to do, and the work is to release tension and become very quiet. The vast sense of well-being that results from this discipline is worth the effort. Once you've established yourself in stillness, you are established in ultimate Truth, and the experience of richness which pulses within that stillness rises up to become the whole of your experience. Then you have the feeling that all experience—whether it's something you like or something you don't—is truly wonderful. Then you're completely happy, always, no matter what.

No longer is this joy, this richness, just a fleeting thought, one inch above the level of your ordinary life. It is an experience which releases you from all levels of ordinary life and allows you to live in the extraordinary. Yes, some people in your life may still be difficult, and yes, they may make you cry from time to time, and you will feel sadness when people—your family as well as strangers—try to get you down. But the difference now will be that the difficult people won't get you down—not in any way you can't handle. Just stay quiet long enough to starve all the tensions which come up in your mind; do this on a consistent basis; starve the tensions of the difficult people and every other kind of tension, starve them of their energy by giving energy to "I wish to grow," and you will feel the tensions wither up and fall away.

Systems thinking provides us with some insight here. Put simply, systems thinking sees wholes; it discerns interrelationships rather than separate entities in political, ecological, physiological, corporate, organizational, whatever systems. Systems thinking discusses patterns of change—the notion that what a person does in one place within a system will invariably alter that system in ways that may not be foreseeable. Systems thinking examines feedback concepts, those having to do with change and those which preserve the status quo.

In systems thinking, the negative feedback loop in the dynamic system that is a human being is the mind; it's anything you think at all. The mind strives to keep everything just as it is and you and everybody around you just as they are. As we will discuss further in Chapter Eight, this is why the ultimate goal of meditation is a thought-free state, a place where, like the highest form of mantra, there is no syllable. Through meditation, you reach within yourself and beyond your mind in order to digest finer and deeper experiences, in order not to be limited by anything which tells you that you must be this or that. Then there's nothing to think about; it's just a question of feeling and feeling—again not "feeling" in any saccharine sense of the word, but feeling into the depth of the Self. If you think and think, you're only going to be confused.

Tensions only have life in them when you don't feel deeply enough into your Self—in other words, when you are thinking instead of feeling.

So, basically, you must quiet your mind as much as possible and not get frustrated if this takes time. With practice, it will become easier. Cultivate a strong center and the awareness of the flow within you. This will allow you to start over continuously as you meditate if your mind decides to drift off. Just come back to center, find your mantra, and start again.

It's important, though, that you understand that quieting the mind by repeating a mantra is not the same as suppressing thoughts. You do not meditate to suppress fears, doubts, your ambivalent feelings about yourself, or anything else. You meditate to change, truly to change, all of it—to release tension, not to suppress it. Without real change, nothing real happens. When you sit down and ask to grow, there is definitely a way to do it which suppresses tension and another way which releases it. It's a subtle difference. As you practice, you will see the difference and be able to tell when you're suppressing and when you're releasing tension.

Don't jam down on anything; don't suppress fear, doubt, anger, and so on. When you reach through the veil of these tensions to the deepest part of you, to the flow, and you connect to that flow, the result is release. First, surrender everything as deeply as you can, then open, flow, contact the Presence that transcends you. You'll find that you don't suppress anything in this state, not even things as simple as sounds and smells.

Now, how do you reach through your tensions to this finer place so that you are releasing and not suppressing tension? The answer is simple: Work with love. Open your heart and do your work with love. Instead of sitting down and insisting, "Oh, I'm going to tear myself into shreds and destroy this thing I don't like and ignore that thing I can't stand," just relax, be happy, and work with love. If you can't love yourself, love your teacher or your practice or the possibility of change, but work with love. If you work with love, you won't become entangled in your tensions.

If you spend a few years—not just a few hours or minutes, but a few years—in that state of clarity which comes from reaching through your tensions, you will find that your whole nervous system becomes refined. Your range of perception and creative expression expands. But it takes practice, over and over again over time. To put it in a mundane way, you become smarter as you practice. Your capacity for processing input appropriately and skill-fully, delicately manifesting some appropriate output, is increased exponentially.

For example—and this has happened in my experience many times with people in varying professions—I may decide to encourage one of my students who is, let's say, a musician to attend medical school instead of continuing in music. At first, this student may tell me there's no way he or she can become a doctor. She's an artist—not a doctor. I don't push it. She practices her meditation for a few years, and one day says that she's applied to medical school. But she's still skeptical: The entrance exam was tough, she's not sure if she has a "scientific" brain, and so on. When she does well on the exam, wonderfully in medical school, and winds up being, in some cases, rather celebrated in her field, I just smile.

If you're connected to the deepest part of you, there's no such thing as what you are and aren't, what you can and cannot do. What you are is wise, what you are is aware, what you are is connected to the highest form of universal intelligence, and from that state, you can do things you never dreamed of. But it takes time. It takes commitment. Open your heart deeply and the flow of love you feel will lead you through your veil of tensions and dissolve it, dissolve your scars, and open up a whole new world to you—medicine, music, anything, everything—and beyond.

In meditation, there's a chakra, an energy center, at the center of your chest, and this is what we're referring to when we talk about opening our hearts to the flow, which in turn opens up a new world for us. As you'll see later in this chapter, during the guided meditation, you can focus on the heart chakra and expand it, opening it profoundly as you sit. But don't wait for a guided meditation to cause you to open your heart. Begin your meditation, and every minute of every day, with your heart as open as possible and with as much love in that heart as you can muster. This will allow you to leave self-absorption behind and to work from the flow within you. Your awareness of that flow and its expansion will take you right out of your body and beyond your issues into an understanding of the Self, of Vital Force, which has no tensions, no problems, no anxiety, no issues, no limitations, no disease, no nothing. It has only pure, infinite awareness and great joy as its qualities.

In addition to the heart chakra, there are other chakras you will feel during your inner work, and as your work expands, you will be aware of these energy centers every moment of every day. In the guided meditation in this chapter, you will focus on the major chakras located in the base of your spine, in the area of your sex organs, in the abdomen, the heart, the throat, the forehead, and the crown of the head. Focus on keeping these chakras open and flowing at all times—not just when you meditate. In that flow, deep well-being resides.

The chakras are junction points in the various meridians which sustain your physical presence and the function of your mental faculties. They are junction points in the energy mechanism. The chakras themselves are not physical, as the meridians in a discipline like acupuncture are. Instead, they are the junction points where a subtle energy becomes condensed and distributed.

To illustrate: I once lived on the island of Martha's Vineyard near a little fishing village called Menemsha. Outside the village is a salt water pond connected to the

Atlantic Ocean by a sand spit, and in the sand spit is a channel. The pond is a part of the Atlantic Ocean, and depending upon the time of year, the tides, and the various forces of nature, the actual structure of the pond changes as the ocean is redistributed in the pond through the channel. Like the ocean, Vital Force, too, becomes condensed in ponds known as human beings, and the system of chakras in human beings is the energy mechanism, the channel, through which Vital Force moves, changing the structure of the human pond as it does so. If the channel is not open, the pond becomes smaller and smaller; if the channel is free-flowing, the pond expands.

Chakras are the transition points between a subtle and vast vitality—the God in you, Vital Force—and one of its physical manifestations, the human being.

When you first start meditating, sometimes you may not be able to feel all the chakras. But if you persist and move your awareness through these areas, eventually you'll be able to feel a great deal in them, around them, and beyond them. The same is true of your breath. The breathing we use in meditation, which eventually becomes the only way you'll want to breathe, is deeper than the shallow breathing most adults have come to use. The breathing in meditation comes from below your diaphragm, from your abdomen. If you can't breathe from that area right away, don't get frustrated. Simply focus your attention on your abdomen and how you wish to breathe, and eventually you'll take all your breaths from that deeper place. Breathing from the abdomen is natural. When we're born, we all breathe from our abdomens; as we get older, trauma and stress make us take shallower breaths. As your tensions break up, your breath will come more easily, and every part of you will be open and alive.

During meditation, your legs may fall asleep, your nose may itch, your mind may wander, any number of distractions may present themselves to thwart you in your efforts. The little self just has to protest a bit when it's being asked to learn new tricks. But it's okay. Try not to become too distracted by any of it. Just quiet your mind, take a deep breath, and start over again, opening the chakras one by one, as the guided meditation will teach you.

Ideally, you will meditate twice a day for about forty-five minutes at each sitting, but be tolerant of yourself if, in the beginning, the only thing you can manage is once a day for half an hour. It's best not to have eaten just before you meditate. Don't make your body digest food while you're trying to transcend the body. Sunrise, at around 6 AM, and sunset, around 7 PM, are good times to meditate, as is the noon hour. Daily practice is important because through it, you build composure, centeredness, openness, which will make it possible for you to cut through your own tensions and the tensions of those around you.

Set up a regular practice, but don't become tense about your discipline by thinking in terms of rules and prescriptions. The boundaries of when to meditate, where to meditate, and so on serve only to keep you in balance. If you make them into another tension, then what's the point? Once you've awakened the power within you and expanded it through your inner work, the work will become so compelling, you'll look forward to meditation. Then there won't be anything to remember; you won't be tense over any of it. It will be something you do automatically and can't wait to do.

In addition to meditation, there is an exercise you can do to release tension at any time of day. It's a simple exercise: Sit in a chair with your feet planted firmly on the floor and your arms draped over the arms of the chair, your hands dangling freely; or if the chair has no arms, hold your arms away from your sides, allowing them to dangle freely in the space about six to eight inches from your sides. Feel the tensions of your day drain away down your arms into the air and down your legs and feet into the ground.

Practice this tension-release exercise as often as you like but at least once or twice a day, for ten to twenty minutes at a time. Do this before meditation, and your sitting will be more productive: You will come to meditation more tension-free; this in turn will allow you to spend more time with the Self and less time trying to get there.

I remember when we first started the ashram in Bloomington, Indiana years ago, someone might be having a discussion with someone else, and if one person got tense in the discussion, that person would continue talking with their arms out at their sides. Of course, that just made everyone tenser. You can do the tension-release exercise in the company of other people, but try not to do it all over someone else's attempt to communicate with you. Just as silt builds up at the mouth of a river, so tensions accumulate in everybody, and you don't want to be dumping your silt on someone else. After all, in releasing tension, you're hoping to facilitate flow in your environment, not dampen it.

In addition to the tension release exercise, do some form of physical exercise on a consistent basis throughout your week. Also, get enough sleep and pay attention to your diet. By this, I don't mean, be a vegetarian, or anything in particular. Just be aware of the effect your diet has on you and make whatever adjustments are necessary for it to enhance your sense of total well-being.

Finally, there are two other valuable tools you can use to dispel tension. The first is humor. Keep everything appropriately light, keep the space inside yourself as light as possible. At the end of the day, laugh at yourself and the idiosyncrasies of your life. It's only when you struggle to make sense of it all that you get into serious trouble.

However, I'm not saying you should become a stand-up comedian in every situation, not just because it may not be your calling but also because, and this brings us to our second valuable tool—constraint—all that talking will disperse a lot of your energy in an unproductive fashion. Cultivate the habit of talking less. Don't make yourself crazy with self-examination, but do give some thought as to whether or not the thing you're about to say really needs to be said. Remember, that's important energy you're giving away out of your mouth. Make sure it will be of real benefit to you and everyone before you give it.

Constraint is in fact one of the methods we use to shift our state. When you feel bummed out or agitated, instead of picking up the phone and calling your best friend and telling him all about your woes, which will only give those woes energy, try sitting still and being quiet. The mood will become more and more intense at first—that's fine. Just stay quiet. Do the counter-intuitive thing. Be still. In about twenty minutes, the agitation or depression or panic or whatever tension will reach a point of maximum density. Stick with being quiet. Don't lose your head and start running around the room or opening your mouth. Just stay quiet. Move around a bit if you have to, but be as still as possible in mind, heart, and body. The tension will release. Then when you do get up, you'll feel much better, and you probably won't want to talk or move around so much anymore.

And if you're in the company of people, and they're trying to drag you into wasting your energy by talking or jumping up and down? Change the way you relate to your environment. In our discussion about the teacher as an energy source, we established that for you to change state, energy is necessary. You must make more energy available at a different frequency within you in order to shift from dwelling in anxiety to living from the well-being within you. That's why being quiet is a good thing because in those silent moments, all your energy is available for your growth—none of it is being syphoned off.

So in a social or work situation, when you need to make a shift, you must create a different interaction with your environment which allows you to pull up more energy from within you. Look for something simple through which to make this happen. For example, how much energy does it take to smell a rose at a critical moment or to admire a green plant that someone in your office might have on their desk? Not much. And you can do this without cutting anyone off. Instead of getting caught up in your tensions or anyone else's, smell the metaphoric rose, see the transparency of the figurative green leaves. With a smile on your face, quiet the inside of you even as you're standing in front of a crowd of people, eyes open, hearing acute.

The things which get you all stirred up are usually the things from which you need to step back. Look again and again and see if there isn't a different way to deal with the issue. You might want to think about it like this: The things which get you the most stirred up are the turning points in your life. Therefore, these situations are not a disaster, they're really wonderful; and these points are the most important times to stay quiet within yourself, fully surrendering the little self's agenda as much as you can. Your chemistry will be aroused, you'll think the situation is impossible, but it's not. This is the time to bring in all the important parts of your practice and to remember that your energy has to go somewhere, so it might as well go into releasing limitations and existing strains rather than into reinforcing them. This is how you take compression and use it to increase flow, to uplift, to transform. Increasing flow is easy when you're feeling expansive. The real work is to do it under pressure. But you can do it. You can.

Compression is part of life. It's part of any endeavor, creative, spiritual—any endeavor. In compression, there's a lot of input, most of it discordant. It's coming at you from every direction. Compression is necessary because often it comes in the form of feedback, from other people and from ourselves. It tells us how we're doing. It indicates a dissatisfaction with something from within ourselves, our audience, or the broader field of our lives. Open to the compression. Absorb it. Don't avoid getting compressed. Don't stand away from it and say, "I'll open over here where everything's pleasant and beautiful, but I won't open over there because things are too rocky there."

Instead of reacting to the compression by thinking, "Oh, this is bad, and I need it to be different," or "I'm a bad person," or "This is a bad situation," just open yourself up, relax and remember that compression is useful. Allow the event to settle. Continue to breathe deeply. Stay out of your head and allow your chemistry to go through the transformation it's seeking based on the nature of, the energy of, the feedback. Don't disconnect from the feedback; listen to the feedback you attract. When you find you've gotten overly confident or your life is giving you some feedback to that effect, don't get overly down on yourself either. Swinging between arrogance and self-castigation is meaningless. Just bring yourself back to center, internalize the feedback, and allow it to transform you.

Allow feedback to be structured through the value system and the principles by which you now, as a growing person, live your life; allow the feedback to be structured through surrender, calmness, and virtue.

So from our discussion of the use of compression, breath, chakras, quieting the mind, mantra repetition, and tension release, it's clear there is skill involved in inner work. There is a craft to spiritual growth and there is an art, and trying to understand the craft in order to express the art is what your meditation practice is about. But if you don't sit down and do the basic work every single day, you will not understand the instrument that you are. You are an instrument, you are an instrument of Divine Force, and if you don't understand the instrument that you are, you will never get past it to the Force Itself.

The Force Itself is love, and so once again, before we turn to the guided meditation, I will say: Work with love. If you want something special to happen in you, it's going to take a real and strong commitment. By working with love, this real commitment is not a contraction. The work itself may be a constraint, but because of the love, there is an underlying expansiveness, a joy which will keep you from getting stuck in your tensions. Work with love and allow that love to expand in you, to reach into the sinew and marrow within you and become the vibration of your very nervous system—a vibration which reaches out everywhere and always at once.

A GUIDED MEDITATION

Ordinarily, when you meditate on your own, you will probably keep your eyes closed. But until you've learned how to meditate, you may want to keep your eyes open and this part of the book in front of you as you sit. That way, you can easily follow the instructions. Position the book at eye level, not on the floor. Your chin should be raised so that the flow of your breath isn't cut off in your throat.

Allow an hour for meditation. This will give you the opportunity to become deeply relaxed and quiet and to release the tensions in each chakra. If you complete the guided meditation in less than forty minutes, simply continue to meditate, feeling the energy move through each of the chakras, releasing tensions more deeply as you go.

Sit up straight on a cushion that's high enough to cross your legs comfortably in a full or modified lotus position, or if you're sitting in a chair, sit with both feet flat on the floor. Close your eyes. Put your thumbs and forefingers together with your hands, palms up, on your thighs, right hand on your right thigh, left hand on your left thigh.

Relax your shoulders. Pull them back and drop them. Relax your upper arms and forearms. Clench your hands tightly for a moment, tense your arms completely, release them, and feel the tensions flow out and the energy move through your arms and hands. Do this several times. Relax your legs, tensing the muscles and then releasing them. Do this a few times. Feel your entire body relax in the process.

Pay attention to your breathing. Breathe in a regular, relaxed way. As you breathe in and out, notice the pulsation in the base of your spine as the base moves forward on the out-breath and back on the in-breath. This rocking motion is the pulsation of creative energy. If you do not feel this rocking motion at first, don't be concerned; just bring your attention to the base of your spine and let it remain there.

191

As you continue to breathe, draw the breath directly to the base of your spine; as you become aware of the rocking motion, synchronize the breath with it. Again, if you don't feel the rocking motion, that's fine; continue to bring your attention to the base of your spine and your breath.

Take a deep breath from your abdomen. Exhale slowly. Relax your body. Concentrate on the simple pulsation at the base of your spine; feel a subtle shift take place in that chakra. When you feel that shift, move your attention a little higher into the area of your sex chakra. If you do not feel the shift in the chakra at the base of your spine, continue to stay quiet. You have plenty of time to feel into each chakra for a shift to take place. What you are feeling for is a release of tension in each chakra as you focus on it. At first, it may be a very small release. If you do not feel it right away, that's fine. Just stay quiet and focused, and when you are ready, take your attention higher, into the sex chakra.

As you focus on each chakra, do not strain to make any release happen or to think that a release must happen.

That creates more tension. Breathe, relax, stay quiet, and move your attention from one chakra to the next when you feel you have focused and released as much as possible.

Now breathe through the sex chakra to the base of the spine, synchronizing your breath with the pulsation of creative energy at the base of your spine as you breathe deeply into the sex chakra. Once you feel the subtle release of tension in the sex chakra, take your attention into the chakra in your abdomen, which is about two fingers below your navel. Feel that point. Tighten your whole abdomen. Tighten your stomach muscles as tight as you can and release. Take a deep breath all the way down into your abdomen, fill it up, and then exhale. Tighten your abdominal muscles again, very tight; release; take another deep breath into your abdomen and relax.

Feel that central point around which the tensing just happened in your abdomen. That central point about two fingers below the navel is the abdominal chakra. When you feel anger, or sometimes when you feel fear, that point in the pit of your stomach tenses. That tension is the crystallization of the energy in that chakra. Take your awareness into the chakra and release the crystallization.

Take another deep breath into your abdomen, hold it; allow the energy to expand there, and as it expands, feel your attention naturally rotate upward to the center of your chest into the area of the heart chakra. Feel an expansion in your whole chest and exhale. Relax your body. Whenever you become aware of any tension anywhere in your body, relax that tension.

Take your attention into the area of the heart chakra and breathe naturally, synchronizing your breath with that basic pulsation in and out of the heart chakra. Become aware of the point at which the breath is fully extended before it begins to be retracted, or, conversely, be aware of the point where the breath is fully contracted before it begins to be extended again. As you breathe in and out, be aware, at the end of the out-breath, of a quiet. In that quiet, relax yourself completely. Relax in your heart chakra very deeply every time you breathe out. Become aware of the tensions in your heart, and relax them more deeply with every out-breath.

Breathe and fill your whole chest cavity. Breathe in fully and completely until the breath stops. Hold it. Feel an expansion across your whole chest. Hold a little longer. Slowly exhale. Take a deep breath again, exhale and relax. Be aware that your heart is now open.

Swallow. Relax your throat. In harmony with the pulsation of creative energy extending itself from the base of your spine through your cerebrospinal system, breathe into and through your throat. On each out-breath, relax your throat, and feel an expansiveness there. Be aware of the subtle vibration that is the throat. Swallow in your throat to relax. Feel the channel of the chakras as it extends from the base of your spine through your sex chakra into the abdominal chakra up into the heart chakra and into the throat. Breathe deeply, focusing your attention on the creative energy pulsating in the channel of the chakras, while feeling into the throat for a release of tension there.

When you have experienced the release, breathe up through your nose into the center of your head. Become aware of a point between and slightly above your eyebrows. Breathe through it to the center of your head and relax your whole head. At the end of each out-breath, relax and feel the pulsation of creative energy from the base of your spine through your sex chakra, your abdomen, your heart, your throat, into your head. Breathe deeply, exhale, relax your whole head, and be aware of this creative flow. Breathe in through the point between your eyebrows and be aware of the energy flowing down through the chakras from the point between your eyebrows. Feel it flow from the point between your eyebrows through the throat, the heart, the abdomen, the sex chakra, to the base of the spine on the in-breath. Then feel the energy flowing up the spinal column through the center of your head on the out-breath. Experience this flow going down the front and up the back.

Continue to be aware of your breathing. At the end of each out-breath, relax yourself completely, and be aware of a deeper opening taking place within you, a state in which you are physically relaxed, mentally quiet and calm, emotionally very simple and open. Feel the natural pulsation of your creative energy. Feel the flow.

Now, imagine a very large ball of white light above your head. Breathing regularly and relaxing on the out-breath, take your attention to that ball of white light and look at it. With each breath, feel a simple sweetness pulsating from the ball in waves as the sweetness flows down into your head, over the sides of your head and down the front. Be aware of the sweetness moving into your throat. Swallow in your throat and relax. Feel the sweetness moving into your heart. Take a deep breath there, relax, allow this flow of sweetness to fill your heart. Breathe into your heart to make more room and allow the sweetness to fill you deeply. As this very sweet energy fills you up, feel it overflowing from around your heart, down into your abdomen. Feel it flowing through the chakra in your abdomen into the sex chakra. Be aware that it is flowing to the base of your spine. This sweetness opens you deeper still.

As it pools at the base of your spine, slowly be aware of this fine, sweet energy beginning to rise up the base of your spine. Feel it move slowly in harmony with the pulsation of creative energy in your breath, as a wave extending itself from this large and beautiful ball of white light all the way down to the base of your spine and back up again.

Relax the crown of your head. Relax the chakra between and slightly above your eyebrows. Be aware of the opening in the crown of your head extending itself through your whole forehead. Your forehead is now very open. Feel the complete channel of the chakras from the top of your head to the middle of your forehead to your throat into your heart, your abdomen, into the sex chakra, and into the base of the spine. Feel the interconnectedness of the chakras as this simple, sweet energy pours into you, washing through and nourishing you very deeply.

You are in a very relaxed, open, deep and simple state of completeness. Be aware of how totally well you feel. Allow that feeling of well-being to expand. Relax your body. Relax your shoulders. Pull your shoulders back as far as you can without straining and drop them. Take a deep breath and exhale. Relax your neck, your back, your legs.

Take a deep breath and exhale again. With your breath, feel one last time the flow of creative energy pulsating within you. This creative energy is infinite potential, filled with treasure and miracle. It uplifts you and benefits the lives of all those whose lives touch yours.

Open your eyes. Stretch yourself. As you move through your day, continue to explore your extraordinary, spiritual gift.

Having become acquainted with the skills necessary to meditate, we must remember that being technically skilled in any field is not enough. We need to have an authentic sense of what we will do with the skill we develop. Technically proficient musicians may be interesting to listen to, but they're not inspiring. The work of technically proficient artists may be interesting to look at, but it isn't inspired. All the meditation in the cosmos won't do us any good if we can't use it to lead an inspired life. Don't forget why we're doing this.

Simply put, we meditate to love.

Spiritual practice is drawing our energy and our senses more deeply within ourselves. It is a constraint we place on ourselves for the purpose of generating a vision within us of what we can become. Spirituality lies beyond thoughts or conceptual mind; it is higher and finer than the state in which most of us exist now. In other words, the purpose of inner work is to change our state and, in the changing, to have a sense of how that state may act itself out in the world. Hopefully, that acting out will be with love. Working without love, living a life in which expressing love is not primary, is the same thing as playing at the Game of Life we talked about in Chapter One: Play that game, lose that game. Living a life of love isn't just an option, it's essential because the alternative is a lose/lose proposition.

Generating a change of state in our nervous systems through meditation has nothing to do with the attainment of some kind of ecstatic state which has the potential to manifest as hysteria. It is a change in our nervous systems which speaks to the whole universe of our contact with Divine Force, with the energy of Life Itself, with Unconditional Love. Our practice demonstrates a commitment to manifesting that energy in a balanced fashion from the finest, most refined place we can reach to and live from in the Self. The reason we sit, the reason we meditate every day, is first to find the love in ourselves, and then as that love grows, to manifest it in everything we do. Love and highest best interest are the same thing.

Spiritual practice comes down to something very simple: Relax and be happy. Love your life. Love the life you have right now, not the life you hope to have or the one that someone else has. Love the life you have because, for starters, if you don't love it, nobody else will. And if you don't love it, it can't grow beyond where it is today.

This is a total event. It's not that we change here and forget change over there, change this, but don't change that. It's a total event. The dynamics of our lives—what we "do" and what we "be"—must support our transformation, and we pull it off by being willing to sit down often and regularly in order to reach through the tensions and patterns and desires and struggles to a place within ourselves where we are authentically loving and real. That is what the transformation is about: the place in each of us which is authentically loving and real. And we stay there long enough to become nothing but that.

This is not about loving somebody else. This is authentically loving our lives, Life Itself, everyone and everything, including and especially, ourself and our Self. This is about loving God, and God is not "other" than each of us. When we love God as Creative Energy, as Love Itself, as Life Itself, as the deepest part of us, then the possibility exists that we will at last feel God loving us back. That's when the miracles start happening; that's when we feel really happy; that's when our whole perspective changes because we're no longer hunkered down trying to protect ourselves against life. We realize the oneness of everything—self, Self, God, life, Life, everything. Suddenly, we realize Life loves us. We love it. It's amazing. We realize in that moment a total unity between what's inside us and the potential which is expressing itself all around us.

So stay relaxed, be happy, love your life. Relax so that you can truly feel the love inside you and around you. If you keep doing that—really doing that—every day, you will begin to live from a state which is truly exalted. And you will find coming out of you qualities and capacities you never imagined were possible for any human being. Again, there's no cookbook. I can't say, you'll have this quality, you'll gain this capacity. And anyway, all your qualities and capacities will change again and again over time. Just surrender, open to the infinite potential that exists within you, and embrace the many surprising gifts that await you along the way.

The sixty-four volumes of tantras—verses written from the second century B.C. to the twelfth century A.D.

in North India—articulate a unified, systematic view of Reality which boils down to one thing: Relax, be happy every day, love your life. In Chapter Eight of this book, when we discuss Self-realization, we'll come to a more sophisticated understanding of "Relax, be happy, love your life," but the essence of that chapter and of all those ancient Indian volumes still is one simple thing: Stay in the moment, heart open, mind open, in total contact with Divine Presence right here and now. Empty your mind, your heart, and become aware of that Presence. Live in It, live from It, live in and from Its love.

Empty yourself of your self so that your work, within you and in the world, is a loving tribute to the whole, the One. Then nothing else matters and tension has no reality. When you are loving, you are open, tension-free; anxiety simply is not possible; you are happy. And when you are happy, you are doing the most important thing to make this world a better place in which to live: You are putting your meditation into action.

WITH OUR EYES OPEN

Meditation in Action;

Living in the World,

Sustaining Inner Work,

Working through Resistance

SO LET'S SAY you're meditating once or twice a day, relating to family and friends on a calmer level. Still, there's the world "out there." How do you put your meditation in action as you move through your day, encountering all kinds of people, dealing with your boss, with co-workers, meeting varied demands? After all, unlike your family, people at work have no real motivation to try to love you or even to like you, and in the workplace, if you're not deemed "lovable," you can be replaced all too quickly.

In addition to your boss and fellow employees, you may have unreasonable clients with whom to contend. They may pressure you with tactics like: "Your competition does everything you do in half the time and for one-third the money; won't you do that, too?" Probably the competition doesn't do what they say, but you want the account, so between you and the client, you create a pot-boiler for yourself.

If you must work in a cutthroat business environment, try not to get too caught up in the wrong kind of under-standing. If you do, you'll be consumed by it. Handling business tensions is no different from handling any other tensions. It begins with you, and sincerely, it can end with you, even when others seem to have the upper hand. If you relate in a business environment as in every other environment we've discussed—with love and respect, calmness and virtue, from the biggest and deepest part of you that is being cultivated by your daily meditation prac-tice—the event that is your life in the world will be trans-formed right along with the rest of you.

We do not call inner work, "practice," for nothing. The word, "practice," comes from a Greek word meaning "concerning action." Our spiritual work is active, not some impractical exercise for people who have withdrawn from the world. By doing our work every day and carrying the principles of it into our daily lives, we are changed profoundly. Then, whether we're sitting in meditation or standing in front of a roomful of people, we are the essence of calmness and virtue—the essence of meditation in action.

Some of you may be thinking that I can't know how difficult it is to work in the world, how important it is to have a job and keep it just to survive. You may be saying, "He's a spiritual teacher; what can he know about the harsh realities of the world?"

But I do know and understand. Rudi lived in the world and so do I. The tradition from which my lineage comes does not advocate eschewing the things of this world. I do not live in a monastic cave or on top of some remote mountain, although I think we all sometimes wish we did. I live in the world, just as you do. But I do not let the things of this world eat me alive. In our community, we've been involved for years in business because we understand, and have always understood, that no one is going to make our living for us. One thing we've come to know from years as owners and operators of a successful vegetarian restaurant and a bakery, as well as other enterprises, is that if you produce a quality product, it will attract its own audience and sustain itself.

You may not make a lot of money producing your quality product, but you'll be able to make a very decent living from it, and as important, you'll have a sense of integrity and satisfaction, a strength in your position, which is basically unassailable. Whether you are a creator of ideas or are making something to sell, you're the producer of a product. Think carefully what you need to change to stay competitive while not compromising quality, and then focus on it. If you do your work well, you will earn people's respect.

Some people, however, seem incapable of respect—they just are obstinate and irrational and try to make trouble simply because they can. If it's your boss or somebody you just can't ignore, then you have to endure it, but you don't have to let your mind and emotions get locked on any of it. You don't have to dislike anyone or get mad.

Learn instead to be more skillful when dealing with such people. Project through and beyond the circumstances and keep your focus on the great product you're trying to produce. See if any improvements in the quality of that product can be made. Even though some people may seem irrational, they may have ideas worth incorporating. Look at the way you operate. Does anything need changing?

If you have to be right all the time, then there's no possibility for improvement or living a life of virtue. Virtue arises from your capacity to recognize your personal limitations and go beyond them, and skill comes from having the ability to look at yourself over and over again while thinking about how you can do whatever you're doing better. From that point of view, you can be grateful to your detractors for their comments. But the key is to project beyond any momentary tensions to the highest potential in the situation. This you do by considering the connection between your interests and those of other people.

In the process of having unsatisfactory experiences, you can learn a great deal. If you get upset with other people or with yourself, then there's very little you're going to learn; but if you keep working and working deeply within yourself to stay open, then you *will* learn, even from difficult people, and you'll stop bumping into walls, stepping on other people's toes—even the irrational people's toes—and putting your foot in your mouth. You'll begin to develop a sensitivity and skill with words and a largeness in your understanding which allow for all people, even the difficult ones, to operate in a productive way within the environment.

In creating any kind of project, you need to have an idea of where you're going; you work with an end in sight. So if you start out with a plan in which you're trying to satisfy your ego, you'll end up exactly where you started—with an ego trip. But if you want to make something of quality, you'll begin with quality, and that means you'll work at your business the same way you work in your practice—your focus will be on growth, yours and your company's, and that growth will manifest in everything you do. So you begin with a sincere concern for everyone involved, and then whatever happens will have the best chance of being of quality and of wide benefit.

Every business environment is different, every person in that environment has his or her own concerns. But how to deal in the world is the same as how to deal with anything we've discussed before: Forget your attachments to a particular outcome; focus on the best interests of your group and from there to the highest best interest of the whole. In other words, focus on quality, inner and outer. After that, you just can't be attached to how it works out.

For example, if you want to open a restaurant and serve quality food, you need satisfied customers and cheerful employees. To arouse in people a sense of satisfaction, you have to give the customer quality, even exceeding his expectations, and you need to give your employees or co-workers an environment in which they can serve the customer well. This means the ingredients you use must be fresh; the ambiance, both in the restaurant and in the kitchen, appealing; the presentation, inventive, attractive. The right attitude has to prevail in every area of the operation; if it does, producing quality work will be more important to you than making lots of money.

But if you're not concerned with quality and are thinking only of dollars and cents, fame and fortune, or whatever the self-absorbed goal is, then you may not care about any of the things we've mentioned. This will be obvious to the customer and the people who work with you. And so the feedback you get, in the long run, won't be the feedback you want. In the short-term, things might work fine, but as time goes by, the negative feedback from people who want and know quality will lock you into a shabby event that's self-perpetuating. If the time ever comes when you want to change the restaurant into something finer, you probably won't be able to turn it around.

We all have to have the courage of our convictions, we have to act in accordance with our values of calmness and virtue. Sometimes we get so caught up in the doing of something, our values, which were the original force behind the event, evaporate. But we can't let this happen; we can't let the event itself justify all kinds of scuzzy actions in which our set of values suddenly switches. At that point, instead of being internally driven, we're externally driven; instead of using our vision to create something special, we're in it for the money.

To express a vision of quality and substance, we must set aside something like money as the motivation and guard against overextending our vision. Bigness is such an American concept, but it's potentially dangerous. Better to have a vision geared to quality and manageability than to have a dream of being huge. Your inner work will help you dig out from within you the fineness you wish to manifest, and it will show you, in turn, how to manifest it.

When you don't care about quality, you're playing the Game of Life again, and remember the rule: Play, lose. Losing is what always happens when desire supersedes true caring.

So best to start out on the front side caring about quality. If you start every day in everything you do with a sense of service to Life—which is where you'll always start if you're deeply connected to the finest part of you— and if you make your work an act of love and devotion, then both positive and negative feedback will expand any event in a productive way. You'll hear the customers griping and your employees groaning in time to make your restaurant something which reflects your integrity and at the same time provides you and those who work for you with a very reasonable living.

Putting your meditation in action is quite simple really. You get in the rhythm and flow of whatever work you're doing—restaurant, sales, publishing, factory work, whatever. When you know you're part of that rhythm and flow, shift your attention inside. Observe the rhythm and flow inside, too. Then breathe your inside flow into the outer flow of the event and feel a sense of joy about it. When you shift your attention from outer to inner, you'll find you can draw in the physical energy of your work or any activity and circulate it. As you do, you'll develop a deeper rapport with what you're doing and the people with whom you're doing it. You take in energy and you give out energy; a flow carries you. This way, you are in tune with any environment in any given moment. That, in turn, allows you to recognize that you're part of a bigger event.

Don't allow the rhythm of the restaurant, the city, the store, the shop, office, clinic, classroom, whatever, wherever, to dominate your awareness. Even if you work in a place which values you, connect first to the vibration in you and then to the vibration of the place you're in as it exists today, not as it was last week or yesterday or even a few hours ago. A physician doesn't treat a patient from where she has it in her notes the patient's illness was last week. So, too, you have to find the energy of a given moment and open to and become connected to that, to the stillpoint in that. This way, you're not relating to your boss or anyone or anything as you *think* they are based on what you're sure they were. You begin fresh each day and work with a compassion which is current instead of a disrespect which should be past.

When you merge inside and out like this, you're not separating mind from body, spacing out. Instead, you're finding a way to expand into a real event; it is inside you and you are inside it.

I have several friends who are consultants. Most of the people for whom they consult are not as interested in what my friends have to say as they are in my friends' energy, in their flow and vibration, and as long as the clients can take that energy and in some way be reassured from the contact, they feel momentarily stabilized. When a client realizes the value of a consultant's energy, the creative possibility to transform an organization profoundly, or some part of it, exists, and in that process, the consultant also learns much. This is the optimal exchange of energy we always look for in our interactions with the world.

Interaction is, in fact, nothing more than an exchange of energy. So the first question you want to ask is: What in an energy exchange is going to govern the rhythm of it? Is it going to be what you think happened or what they think happened—in other words, a defensive position—

or is it going to be that finer and deeper vibration you know exists inside you as well as whomever you're working with? When you start to understand yourself as energy and reach within to find a deeper rhythm from which to interact with people, everything is changed. Again, there's no cookbook for what this new interaction will look like, but one thing it won't look like is a combat zone.

All relationships are energy fields where material of one kind or another is exchanged, and the material most people exchange is tension. Centuries of family tensions, plus the tensions people heap on themselves daily from a state of ignorance, make it difficult for most people to do anything except pass tension back and forth.

Putting your meditation into action makes it possible for you to stop trading tensions back and forth and to start exchanging finer and finer energies. When you pause to think about it, you'll realize that it isn't really "sharing" your day with someone if all you do is dwell on everything that went wrong, and it isn't being truly "close" to insist on telling your loved ones over and over about some past trauma. Unfortunately, the only thing you're doing in these situations is creating tension by spreading past unhappiness.

Of course, sometimes you have to talk about some not-so-joyful things, but be thoughtful about when and how you do this, and understand that to become the healthiest, happiest person you can be, you have to get rid of tension and not just trade it back and forth. You have to clear yourself as much as possible of tension by doing your inner work deeply and consistently and then by making your outer work a manifestation of your deep inner commitment to growing.

In a competitive environment, you need to recognize the source of power and through whom it flows and cultivate your own connection with that source without kissing anybody's backside or compromising yourself. Be careful not to be drawn down to the level most people want to operate from; focus instead on the long-term interests of your company, and with those interests in mind, deal with whatever short-term issues arise in a straight-up manner, as best you can. Build cohesion and loyalty by communicating and listening, and be up front about anything you consider inappropriate.

In any group situation, you can't allow yourself to become entangled in personal feelings. Drop as many of your defenses as possible, be open and listen carefully. When you relate to people, if you have true caring in your heart instead of the need to be right, then you'll learn from your experiences. You will learn what to react to and not to react to, how to speak with concern for the whole, and ultimately what your goal really is. If your goal really is mutual growth—yours and your company's—something inside will call out for that growth; you'll feel into that call and bring energy to it, which will eventually transform your state to one beyond personal feelings and history. Then your personal actions will contain concern for others, for things beyond the personal.

When you feel into a situation for the purpose of mutual growth, your personal actions arise out of inspiration instead of self-defense. No longer are you defining a territory, some need you think you have, and then defending it against all comers. When a person marks out a territory, it usually means there's not enough energy in the situation to sustain a real opportunity. When you mark out a territory, it means there's not enough direct work in it for you to find a creative opportunity for yourself. In that case, you've shifted from growing, learning, studying, and expanding to defending. That's when you probably need to make a change, give up that territory, leave it; either get a new job, learn some new profession, or make a shift inside yourself from defense to no fence.

In order to grow while living in the world, you have to reach constantly beyond where you are; you have to find opportunities for growing and expanding and working and deepening yourself. Never mind what the other guy is doing. He's being aggressive? She's got everybody on the ropes? You don't have to respond to any of it by defending anything. The challenge of living in the world and having a spiritual practice is not to succumb to the tensions, not to allow yourself to be magnetized to a level in which everyone is filled with anger, hate, ambition. There's no justification, whatever harm has been done or right has been wronged, for getting entangled in that kind of tension. Operate from your deepest Self, and your personal actions will be transformed into something with an energy which functions through you and operates in the highest best interest of the whole your actions are intended to serve.

If your personal actions do not arise from inspiration, then they arise from insecurity and greed—fear and greed—and then they serve no one; you, least of all.

People respect calmness and virtue as a source of personal action because inner strength and its extension to others makes us capable of doing better work and of keeping everybody's interests in mind. It doesn't matter if someone else is acting from self-interest. Just be a person with integrity at home and at work. As we said earlier, you can't justify greed, lust, pride, by saying you're only grubbing for money now so you can be virtuous later. It doesn't work that way. You have to be virtuous now—when it's

not so easy—or you won't be virtuous then—or then—
or then—or ever.

I definitely do understand lures the world dangles in
front of people in every walk of life. For example, as I
indicated before, where inner work is concerned, there is
religion and there is spirituality. If I made religion my
career, the truth—which is that life *is* hard and it's *all*
work, and even states of joy and happiness require work
to achieve—would not be my main focus. If religion
were my career, my desire to make money or be famous
would dominate the truth in me, and I would tell you
anything easy: Without deep inner work, you, too, can be
happy and rich and have everything you want—for a
small donation.

But religion is not my career. I am a spiritual person,
and if I weren't telling you the truth, if I weren't every
single second of every single day coming from the Self
and not the self, then, seriously, very seriously, I'd rather
be gone from here, finished, nada, dead.

We need to try to put every activity the world touts as wonderful in its proper perspective. When we pay attention to what the final result of work in the world is, we realize it's retirement. What does that say about the value of killing yourself to have some thing or to get some place by doing less than exemplary things?

And what's the end of retirement? Death. So what does that say? It says to me that the essence of who we are is far more important than what we do because everything we do is finite whereas essence is forever.

I remember the essence of my teacher in action. One afternoon when I was working in Rudi's oriental art store in New York City, several celebrities stopped by, as they often did. They were making selections of art, talking with Rudi, browsing through various artifacts, when a tiny Jewish lady who lived in the somewhat dilapidated brownstone around the corner came in and said, "Rudi, please, I need…" She began to wander around the store in a daze.

Rudi went over to her immediately. She needed to buy a wedding gift for her grandson, and she only had fifty dollars to spend. Rudi took at least twenty minutes to help her find something she liked for fifty dollars. He didn't ignore his famous clients for her, but he didn't ignore her either. I suspect that what he found for her to buy for fifty dollars actually cost more like five-hundred dollars, but it didn't matter to Rudi. He responded to the real needs of real people in a real, straight-up way—he didn't respond to money or image or notoriety or the potential for more business.

Rudi's actions were the essence of spirituality in action and of a spiritual value system at work which demonstrated its respect for the Creative Energy, God, in all people.

Moving in the world and working without attachment and desire or expectation is the real test of our essence, of who we deeply are. In other words, the real test is our ability to exist in a state of total surrender and complete openness no matter what we get or don't get and no matter who is doing what to whom. The bottom line is that the things of this world are going to dissolve anyway; do the best job you can, be as respectful as you can, and don't get entangled in the tensions along the way.

If it's possible, try to choose a place to work in which people are valued for their efforts and loyalty. In such an environment, the values you hope to cultivate will be reinforced. Of course, there's always something you have to deal with and someone who isn't fully cooperative, and sometimes you'll get ground up in the competition and the pressure, but try to keep your focus on being and not just doing.

We each have a responsibility to compose ourselves before beginning to relate to our environment. When we're composed, real openness and a flow can occur; authentic communication becomes possible. If we try to say something to someone who refuses to hear us, this is usually for one of two reasons: We're not communicating effectively or they're not listening. If it's the latter, drop it; it's not yours with which to deal. If it's the former, do something about it, and try yourself to be one of the good listeners when it's your turn to hear what the other person has to say.

So try working in the world like this: Instead of racing off into your daily activities, pull your attention down from your mind and be truly present. Pull your attention into your center, into your abdominal chakra, and begin to feel the rhythm of your work. Circulate the energy of that work ever more deeply inside you. Don't go off in your mind; stay present. Be connected to the energy as it works you.

That is how we practice when we sit, and that is how we put our meditation into practice as we move through our day. In fact, I teach my students how to meditate with their eyes open. There is no drifting off; we keep our eyes open, stay present, and observe the intricate and sophisticated dynamics which occur as we sit still. As a result of this eyes-open meditation, we're able to observe those dynamics not just when we're sitting but also when we're standing, walking, whatever. Sitting down or not sitting down, we get quiet and stay quiet until we feel everything come into line, and then our hearts open naturally. We may have to stop for twenty-five to sixty seconds a hundred times a day to reinforce our inner alignment, but we do it. With our eyes open, we find the stillpoint in every situation—we find the stillpoint in ourselves—and we work from that.

Remember that in every turbulent circumstance, as well as in quiet moments, whether we're observing nature or our own field of experience, a stillpoint exists. The stillpoint is part of the pendulum of life, it's part of a hurricane, it's part of everything; it's part of us. Every situation has a stillpoint. If we're embroiled in a conflict at work or at home, or wherever, and if instead of losing our composure, we get quiet, centered, focused on the stillness deep within us, then a stillpoint will come up on the horizon of the conflict, and that stillpoint will be like a doorway. If we are still enough in ourselves, we will discover how that doorway presents a way to resolve the conflict.

We've talked a lot about other people's resistance to us. But let's talk for a moment about our resistance to others and to events we don't relish. It's important to understand that if you don't overcome your resistances, you'll increase the inertia in your life. As the inertia builds, you may feel joyless because you become convinced once again of your need for this and that, and when you don't get it, you feel alienated and separate. A kind of quiet hysteria grows inside you which repels calmness and virtue. Then the hysteria becomes not so quiet.

If you resist doing something beneficial, just do it anyway. As the tension of your resistance releases, you'll realize that it's worth the work to reach through the tension on behalf of everyone concerned.

This resistance is not the same as the inertia of not knowing what to do. When you don't know what to do, pause for a moment. Sit down, be quiet, consider the first step, take it. Then think about the next step. Do research if it's appropriate; create a framework, but don't look too far down the road. That way, the first step can create a flow from which all other steps will follow. If you act from a deep place within you, that place will guide you.

Any dynamic event contains a lot of uncertainty, and ultimately, to know something, you just have to take the first step and try it. When you've done your research, considered everyone in your environment, and taken that first step, you also have to accept completely that your best will never be perfect. But since the real issue is the fusion between you and the people you're trying to serve, when the glitches happen, as they inevitably will, you digest everything as part of your commitment to deliver something of quality, and your best, while not perfect, will definitely be more than good enough.

Confronting inertia and pushing through resistance is how each of us encompasses layers of tension in any work environment, be it inner or outer. Whether it's your inner work or your work in the world, this process is what allows you to digest tension as energy.

Let's take an example of pushing through resistance in professional life. Say you're a musician and you have a concert to play. You care about playing; it's central to your Self-expression, and it is your profession, but you'd rather not play this particular concert. It will contain a tough audience, and your past experience in a similar situation was terrible. So you *really* don't want to go out on that stage. You said before you'd never play again under these circumstances, but here you are—the group you play with just is committed to this concert. What do you do? You walk onto the stage, take your place at the microphone, and start playing. You use the pressure on you in the situation to perform better. From that place deep inside you, you pull up the ability to overcome your resistance and play. Even though you're afraid, you reach through the tension, without forcing anything, to the place where you can be calm, deeply focused and centered, and you play from there. Slowly, slowly, you push your way through. You deliver the music.

This is the creative process, which is also what meditation is, and it applies to any profession or activity. This is what your work inside and out is about. This is how you take resistance and turn it into energy with which to grow.

So can you be president of something as worldly as a corporation and have a rich inner life? Yes, if you can put contemplation at the center of your outer as well as inner life. Perhaps there will be a circumstance intrinsic to some positions with some institutions which will prevent you from both leading a contemplative life and working there. But that will be for you to decide. It will be for you to find your value system and stick to it.

At some point, though, in order to choose happiness over a world of need and greed, you're going to have to recognize the benefit of being more contemplative; and you'll have to assert your wish to be contemplative perhaps at the expense of a material dream. Truly, because it affects every phase of your life, the most productive time you spend each day is in contemplation. You have to establish this time and value it, and that may mean you won't progress in the material world to celebrity status. As you come to understand the value of service in your quest to be a loving, happy person, you may also feel some need to make a community contribution on a daily basis, and the energy you spend in that service may mean you won't have the energy to be president of your company.

On the flip side, though, the person whose life goal it is to be president of something may wind up sacrificing ultimate happiness and growth for the sake of money, power and security. As we've already seen, security is an illusion, and all material dreams end in death. As a result, I'd rather spend the energy I have growing as a person and helping others do the same than chasing after something which doesn't exist, like security, or something finite, like power and money. But you'll have to decide for yourself what you'll do.

When you do extend your energy into the world, ask yourself: Who is really doing what? Are you being manipulated and controlled by the structure of your environment or are you doing something truly productive for yourself and others? Is the extension of your energy into the world something you've chosen or something that's somehow been chosen for you by someone else's value system. Are you flowing into it or have you let yourself be led into something just because it's there? In other words, do you really belong wherever it is you are, doing whatever it is you're doing?

To imagine that the cycles of material life prevent us from attaining that to which we aspire is a mistake. The real issue is the degree to which we live in contemplation of the fundamental power of Life within us. This is the guiding principle. If we live from the Self, we will always be rich in what matters. If we live from the Self, what we do in the world will always be an expression of what it's productive for us to do, of that for which our Creative Energy was intended. When we're guided by love, what we do in the world is simply what we do. Then what we do in the world and what we want from the world involve balance, calmness, virtue, rather than some type of quantifiable gain.

If your life is not one of simplicity and unbroken stability, remember you have a choice—we all have a choice—not to choose the roller-coaster ride.

If you choose that ride, it will definitely hold you in your seat; it will hold you to the lowest level. But if you surrender the world while still living in it—rise above its values to live from the values of your true Self—then you'll stop looking for anything from the world. In that case, everything that happens will be an opportunity for your growth; you will have integrity in everything you do because you're no longer fixated on some outcome you think you must have to survive. Instead, you're free to act according to your values; whatever happens, as long as it is a result of those values, you can stand behind it. Then, if the world gives you a kiss, you enjoy it; if the world frowns, that's fine, too.

Stop doubting yourself. Stop rejecting and punishing yourself. Stop worrying about what other people think of you. Do your work, inside and out. Live from your values. Serve to the best of your ability. Stop trying to make sense of the world and of yourself and instead explore the Truth; come to understand your fundamental nature and the nature of all things. That nature is completely free of worry; it is beyond anxiety. That nature strives for nothing except growth. It doesn't fret over money, relationships or any of the things of this world. It surrenders everything because it knows that surrender is the key to being light, free, happy, to living beyond anxiety. It knows that only in a state of surrender can we live from the Truth, from the Self.

Far from giving up anything of real value when you surrender, you gain value because you recover your true Self; you recover joy.

If you live from your biology and chemistry, you may find only two things of value in your life: One will be the food you eat—or the money you need to buy that food (this includes all the appliances and accoutrements to go along with your food, like your furniture, house, and the job you need to buy it all); the other will be your romantic relationships, or to put it bluntly, sex (the type of car you want and the clothes you wear probably will be determined by this). That's it; if what you live from is your chemistry, then absurdly, food and sex will rule your life. It seems fantastic, but it's true. If your chemistry rules, then every opportunity you seek will have little to do with growth and everything to do with eating and reproducing—which are mostly tension.

Interesting, isn't it, that money and romance contain a great deal of tension? This is hard for most of us to see at first because we've been trained to look at jobs and romance as fulfillment. But if we're honest with ourselves, we often find that making money for food and then attracting and satisfying a mate involve a lot of striving and worry. These activities are not *just* tension, but we have to look at how much tension and anxiety they carry with them before we're able to make intelligent decisions about their place in our lives.

Eating and reproducing are what we call the biological imperatives. Our bodies are designed to perform these activities; the body cannot survive without eating; the species cannot survive without reproducing. So it's natural that we place so much store by them; it's programmed into us. But what we're looking for in romantic love and in jobs simply doesn't exist there.

We imagine that some other person can make us happy, can save us from our anxieties, illnesses, depressions, lack of whatever—another person can't; we imagine some major success will make us feel fulfilled for a very long time—it won't. As we already said, other people have their own growth to attend to—they cannot do our growing for us; and jobs end in retirement and death.

Happiness, deep well-being, exists only in the deepest part of us and depends not at all on having anyone or anything outside us. Eating and reproducing are biological imperatives, yes, but the deepest part of us—which is the only place from which happiness can come—requires a whole different kind of food, and each one of us—and only each one of us—is ultimately responsible for feeding that part.

But if we live from biology, eating and reproducing will be the only things commanding us. Think about it: The only things we'll be living for are cookie and nookie; and this is why I'm somewhat skeptical about self-improvement objectives. Many times, self-help is about little more than eating and reproducing. When we take on some program for self-improvement, too often we're trying to gussy ourselves up for the purpose of attracting a job or a mate, not really to improve anything deep in ourselves. Unfortunately, at those moments, we're a bit like the cuttlefish, which changes color and pattern in order to attract something to eat or some other cuttlefish with which to reproduce. For the cuttlefish, changing color in order to eat and reproduce is everything; for us, it doesn't have to be.

Think about it very seriously—because you have a choice—do you really choose to say that the opportunities that are everything to a cuttlefish are everything to you as well?

You probably will have relationships; people who live in the world and work in it have relationships. But the question is: Will finding a romantic partner, and then keeping your relationship afloat, be your focus, or will the finest and deepest part of you be your focus? Where will you put your energy? By all means, have something light and wonderful and companionable in your life. If a relationship does not drain but truly contributes and allows you, as your primary goal, to attend to your growth, entertain such a thing. Have a special relationship with someone you value and respect.

But understand that many relationships create more anxiety in the long-run than the fun can make up for in the short-run and that when you choose to have a relationship, the only thing you're really choosing is another place in which to do very hard work. Unlike holding down a job, which you must do to survive, relationships—after a certain point, even the ones you were born into—are elective. Children, families, are elective and require an enormous amount of energy to sustain. So choose carefully and from a very deep place within you, if you decide to choose.

A relationship is not a life—even when it's a light and wonderful experience, it's not a life. Nothing involving anything outside you is the essence of your Life. Growing—your Self growing—is Life; Life flows from inside you.

None of us has a long time to be here. No matter how young we are, we do not know, nobody knows, how much time he or she may have. So for what purpose is our time here going to be? We have a choice. It truly is up to each one of us. What are our lives going to be about? Changing colors to attract entanglements? Or choosing to live a life of deep growth, of profound change? If we choose the latter, then it's possible for our relationships to be an extension of our essence, of our growth, and as such, we'll be able to contribute to the lives of those around us in a productive fashion. Then tension and entanglement will not be the characterizing qualities of our relating.

If we practice self-deception—if our walk and talk do not match up—then the tensions we create in our relationships will be far greater than if we'd just admitted from the outset that we were in it for the chemistry.

Most things we might wish as entertainment in our lives are usually fine. There's no such thing as purity and impurity. In other words, I'm not suggesting to be cautious about relationships or about desire for money or some high-powered job because sex is a sin or money is evil or all corporate jobs are performed by egomaniacs. But I am saying that we each need to be very honest with ourselves about our capacity to handle what we want. To use, appropriately, a food metaphor, some of us have stronger digestive systems than others. Some of us can consume almost anything with impunity. Others can consume very little without immediately getting indigestion.

Know yourself, know your system, don't overdo the things you have trouble digesting, no matter how good they may look on the surface. If you love chocolate, but every time you eat it, it makes you sick, I imagine you don't eat a lot of it. The same is true of other activities. The real discussion behind pure and impure, good and evil, sinful and sinless is simple: Is the activity in question productive for you or have you been known to gag, perhaps repeatedly, on it?

Not every person is meant to have a relationship—it's perfectly okay not to; likewise, not everyone is meant to be a big, professional success. In fact, true success, true creativity—in other words, God's wish for us—may lie for many of us in some quiet, totally unassuming endeavor. The main thing is, whatever we do and whomever we do it with, our Life should be allowed to unfold Itself from within us. When we allow God, Vital Force, Life, to unfold Itself through us, then we do not confuse our entertainment with our growth.

Life, God, Vital Force is striving in each of us to fulfill Itself, and we, in our pursuit of more, more, more, are the impediments. Our work is to desist from being the obstacles to our own growth; our work is to drop our desire for this job and that person—or whatever desire it is we have—to get out of the way and let Vital Force express Itself through us in everything we do.

Surrender and contemplation, then, are the cornerstones of our worldly activity because without them, we become totally absorbed by and extended into our activities, and then what is outside begins to control us completely. Through contemplation, we begin to recognize an interdependence with people that is not romance or job related, and we develop an inner capacity for a much finer level of exchange. This is true at work; this is true at home.

When we appreciate and respect our interdependence, we begin to treat people in a more compassionate fashion—not because of something we want from them, like romance or a better job, but because we understand that we're all part of the same whole, that the entire team—at work, at home, wherever—is necessary for the success of any project, and we no longer have the perspective that we're so important while someone else is less so. This fundamental understanding takes us a long way toward melting our small selves and its desires. From this understanding, we begin to see the truth: What is sincerely beneficial to someone else may very well be what is totally beneficial for us as well. But to achieve this clarity of purpose, daily practice is essential.

All our opinions about circumstances and judgments about people have to do with our own tensions and limitations in a particular event. When we take away those tensions, what remains is real love.

Every day can be like a treasure hunt. Just because we've looked at the same person a thousand times, interacted with them a thousand times and thought they were a jerk a thousand times doesn't mean that, with the help of our practice, we won't find something very different when we encounter them the thousand and first time. I'm not saying that suddenly we're going to get along with everyone just because we're meditating. But I am saying that as we meditate, our way of relating will be transformed right along with the rest of us, and then we are able to say "no" to someone without closing our hearts or being disrespectful, and we are able to discern the difference between the tensions of our judgments and opinions and the reality of that person standing in front of us.

As growing people, we experience the underlying unity of all things, and our range of creative expression expands as we're transformed into a more universal person, someone who has a sense of connectedness and attunement with all kinds of people, not from a psychological perspective, but from a deeper place—from the perspective that everyone and everything has as *the* source the same Creative Energy. It is all one thing. When we understand this, we see our life is not about what we want—ever; it's about what Life or God wants for us— not *from* us, *for* us. It is about how God chooses to express that Creative Energy through us.

So instead of asking the question, "Can I be president of a big corporation or have a boyfriend or girlfriend and still lead a life of real love and surrender?", begin to think a bit more about something I will call purposelessness.

This doesn't mean being rudderless; it doesn't mean we don't have value for work. Purposelessness is not laziness; it's not being valueless or passive or without goals. In living a purposeless life, we create the environment, mentally, emotionally, psychologically, physically, whereby the deepest and finest part of each one of us can unfold—because a purposeless life is, in fact, a truly inspired life. It is a life in which everything we do reflects the God in us.

Purposelessness does not mean we do not act—that is impossible—but we act in a state of total surrender and only from a joy that is the contact with our deepest essence. To act from that purposelessly and yet in harmony with our total environment is called Liberation. Purposelessness is transcending our physical bodies to live in the complete awareness of Vital Force, which allows for the finest part of us to unfold.

In an environment of purposelessness, the deepest part of us will guide us, and then, being president of a corporation or having a romance may not be too important anymore. What will probably become the most important thing is to know our own essence and to live from that, to surrender consciously every single day everything to God: Everything is already surrendered anyway; why not do it consciously, with love instead of fear and resistance?

The world is not a place God made for us to work out our tensions. God did not make the world for any one of us to be president of anything or to attract anybody. God made the world for each of us to grow.

Anxiety is related to our misunderstanding, which tells us that the life of the cuttlefish is the life for us. But we've seen that it doesn't have to be that way. When we transcend the tensions of our physical bodies and physical lives—when we transcend our desires—suffering dissolves, purposes evaporate, and along with them, anxiety and worries. Then, whatever we do, we do with love and from a deep joy.

8

CHAPTER

THERE IS NO OTHER

Enlightenment,

Self-Realization, Yoga,

And the Choice to Be Happy

OME OF YOU MAY be wondering: "How can we talk about the choice to be happy and at the same time say that the ultimate state in which happiness resides is choicelessness? Those are complete opposites, aren't they?"

I know it sounds paradoxical, but it's not. Ultimately, the way we choose to be happy is by living in deep contact with the Self, and living in that contact over a long period of time leads to Self-realization, which some call Enlightenment. In that state of Self-realization, desire disappears, and all choices are seen as complication, an increase of entanglement or karma, the outcome of which, inevitably, is suffering. Then, for such a person who has this recognition, there is no longer any issue of choice at all; there is no longer any issue of suffering.

This state of Self-realization, or choiceless awareness, is complete bliss, total happiness. So while it is a choiceless state—and the key to real joy—it must be chosen as the focus of our lives.

Now some of your minds may be buzzing: "Enlightenment? Me? I just want to get well or feel good or have a slightly prettier inside; I just want to calm down and learn to relate more productively to my husband, my wife, the kids, or my very difficult boss. Enlightenment? Isn't that for saints or do-gooders? I understand now that leading a spiritual life is possible for everyone and that leading a spiritual life is also leading a happy life. But Enlightenment? I'm just an ordinary person."

I can tell you with absolute certainty: Anyone, *anyone* can achieve the ultimate state of happiness that is Enlightenment, a state beyond desire and suffering. Anyone can achieve Self-realization. You can work in the world, live in it, and be completely liberated. This is the real meaning behind my teacher Rudi's equation of depth over time. Practice long enough and profoundly enough, and suffering will be a nonentity to you; joy, your entire being. Then, all manner of richness on every level will be yours, and whatever it is you feel is important for you to have in your life, you will have. When you live beyond getting or having—when you grow beyond every circumstance—it's very interesting, but everything comes to you.

All richness on every level comes originally from Spirit, from Vital Force. Fulfillment comes on every single level and in every single form from Vital Force. When you live in a state of the full unfoldment of Vital Force—that full unfoldment is the same as Self-realization—and when you trust in that unfoldment and reside in it, your Life becomes complete, rich, wonderful, and everything in your Life sustains itself because it is an expression of the will of God for you. From that state, none of the things in your Life—relationships, work, whatever—none of them are products of the mind's desires; such products, as we've learned, inevitably self-destruct. The degree to which you are able to dedicate yourself to the goal of Self-realization is the degree to which you will experience a profound inner and outer benefit.

But you have to be clear about one thing when your goal is Liberation—you can't be in it for the outer benefit or it's not Liberation. It's just one more thing your mind thinks it needs, and then, like the quest for any object, desire for it will imprison and eventually harm you. Desire is simply the contraction of Creative Energy caused by strain and trauma. When people pursue their desires and have them fulfilled, they are often consumed and destroyed by them because the energy sustaining those desires is the contraction of energy, not the unfoldment of it.

When what is in your life comes from mind, it can destroy;
when it comes from God, it is Life and it sustains itself.

When you understand that Life comes from Vital Force, and you put your energy into establishing your awareness of and trust in Vital Force, then you also trust that everything that is truly required in your life, that Force will give you. When you concentrate on building the skills to allow you to express Creative Energy in a very clear way, everything you can imagine and more will come to you.

To put it simply, when you trust in God, you understand that if it's not in your life, you don't need it; this makes a fool of desire.

So, you do not have to give up anything in your quest for Self-realization; but, yes, you do have to shift your focus once and for all—no half measures, once and for all—to that which is the highest, and then you cannot let *anything* come between you and that. You may find that the things which cause you every kind of suffering, anxiety, and discomfort will drop away from your life. This quest may cost you those things. At first, you may even want to hang onto some of those things: a tense relationship, but at least it's somebody in your life; an even tenser job, but you think you can't leave it because of self-doubt. Your quest for Self-realization may cost you such things as these; but isn't such a cost worth it?

I want to pause here briefly to explain my use of the words "goal" and "quest." You might think that when discussing the achievement of a choiceless state, "goal" and "quest" are inappropriate terms because they imply will, striving, pursuit. In other words, "goal" and "quest" don't sound much like surrender. But in fact these terms do describe the profound determination and intense focus you must bring to bear in your journey toward Self-realization. Pardon me for being crass and using a four-letter word, but the following just is true: Only one thing "just happens;" shit just happens. Nothing of lasting value is accomplished by accident. As we discussed before, even surrender is a state you wish for ardently in your wish to grow; and surrender is work.

So the point is—and it's not a paradox, it only sounds paradoxical—your goal is a goal-less state, and it requires the focus of all your energy to achieve.

That specific state of Self-realization, which is a very definite, palpable state—it is not some mind phase; it is real—has no other goal than the state itself associated with it. It is in fact, without our knowing it—because our tensions hide this from us—the source of all human endeavor and its end. In that state, you want nothing. It doesn't even occur to a person living in that state that he or she needs anything—not a relationship, not a higher paying job, nothing.

However, as we said before, such a person definitely can have relationships, work in the world, be attracted to this person over there, not like that food over here; such a person can and does look just like you and me. He can go to the grocery store, drive a car, buy household items, enjoy something frivolous, whatever. Such a person has not disconnected from reality; she's not out-of-touch, mercifully unbothered by desires because she's no longer playing with a full deck.

Au contraire—the enlightened person has in fact found Reality.

Let us pause here again to explore the meaning of two other important words in this discussion: Enlightenment and Self-realization. They're often used interchangeably, but they're not exactly the same thing. Enlightenment is the state you achieve first. It is a state you can reach into every single day; in that state, you are connected to and live from the Self.

Self-realization is the maturity of Enlightenment. You are still living from the Self, but Vital Force, the Creative Energy, has *fully* unfolded in you. *Full* unfoldment takes more time. It is a result of years of living in the vibrant stillness at the top of the pendulum.

Virtue is also not the same as Enlightenment. Virtue is the extension—not the unfoldment but the extension—of our connection to the Self in terms of our actions in the world. To achieve virtue, we first cultivate the calmness of the Self; from that calmness, we extend ourselves into the world and display virtue. But the actions of virtue are still part of the individual self because we are extending ourselves; in other words, there is still inner and outer. For a Self-realized person, in the full unfoldment of the Creative Energy, there is no longer any distinction between inner and outer—or any distinctions whatsoever, for that matter.

The virtuous person behaves with an awareness of flow and seeks to express, through the actions of the individual self, the highest best interest of the whole. But the enlightened person has transcended even the highest concerns of the individual self; the enlightened person is not locked into any dichotomy, not even into a noble effort, like trying to make the world a better place. The enlightened person has transcended the concerns, high and low, of the individual self and has no concerns whatsoever because his or her Life is a perfect expression of the will of God.

And the Self-realized person? Such a person has transcended the ocean of selves.

It is important to note that while we can discuss Enlightenment and Self-realization to some extent, the states themselves are fundamentally inexpressible in words—the experience of Spirit is fundamentally inexpressible. It is beyond the material world's sight-and-sound show, which words just make denser and more fixed; and since the experience of Spirit is Oneness, how can we talk about gradations of it—this state, that state—and still remain true to what it is? If it were expressible, if it could be captured, limited, and defined by words, then how could it be what it is: the Oneness beyond matter, beyond all limitation? So please understand, we can discuss states and so on, and the discussion can be productive to our journey, but ultimately, if we want to have the experience of Spirit, we must do the work and see for ourselves.

When a person has reached the state of the full unfoldment of the Creative Energy, he or she has practiced long enough and deeply enough that the ocean of diversity has been transcended altogether. Enlightenment may be dipped into from day to day, but Self-realization is a state in which a person swims in the ocean of diversity while permanently living in the deepest contact with Vital Force, which brings perfect clarity. Such a person has completely transcended the ocean of diversity while living in—not from, but in—it.

And what do I mean by the ocean of diversity? The ocean of diversity is the illusion that everything around us is separate from us and from everything else. It is the world of objects and disparate thoughts and seemingly separate beings. It is the world as we think we know it, based on what we see. The ocean of diversity is an illusion because everything actually comes from Vital Force; you come from Vital Force, I come from Vital Force. Even desires have a connection to Vital Force because, as we said earlier, they are powered by the Creative Energy hijacked by a traumatized and tense mind into a contracted state. The mind, the heart, all things are products of Vital Force.

Vital Force is Creative Energy; Vital Force is God.

And so if everything is Vital Force, then everything—contrary to its appearance of diversity—is One Thing. Everything is an expression of one Creative Energy, and so it is an illusion that there is anything "other" than that One Thing. The ocean of diversity is the world of varied appearance—things appear to be diverse and separate; Vital Force is Reality—every thing is actually One Thing.

Within that One Thing, as in a symphony, there are different movements, some of which are more exuberant than others, but it is all part of one Reality.

Now you might be saying, "What am I, then? I'm sure I'm me, and I'm sure that's not the same as being that person over there or that person over there or that tree over there!"

True, you're not that person standing across the room, and you're not the tree outside the window, but that person and that tree still are energy. They have as their source the same Creative Energy from which you come. So you and I and that tree and everyone and everything are simply condensations of that vast Energy known as Vital Force or God. In effect, you and the entire rest of the planet, and the solar system along with it, are effects of Vital Force. Think about it for a minute, and you'll realize that even the simplest, most basic knowledge of the new science of environments and ecologies tells us that all life forms and all environments are interdependent.

Rudi used the analogy of an iceberg to explain how everything is One Thing. He said that a human being is like an iceberg, with ten percent of itself above the surface of the ocean and ninety percent below the surface. And what is an iceberg? It is nothing but a condensed version of the ocean itself. And so what is visible—like your little self and the world and all material things—and what is invisible—like the Self—actually are the same thing in different states.

So if we are all Vital Force, then it is clear that we can all achieve a state of full unfoldment of that Force because it is everyone's natural state to live from and in that Force. It is our natural state to be enlightened and then fully realized. When you understand this, you also understand why it is our natural state to be happy—because with Vital Force fully unfolded, the world of diversity and suffering disappears, and only a bliss remains. Generation upon generation of tension has made us forget this and lose touch with our natural Liberation, and so we meditate to cut through centuries of trauma to our already enlightened, blissful Self.

Thus, meditation is not an end in itself; Self-realization is the goal. In order for the full unfoldment of Vital Force to occur in you, your individual energy must rise as you meditate, and then your energy must continue, in everything you do, to go up. All the energy in you, as it opens, should rise. Rising energy is not the same as energy zipping up the front of you. You circulate the energy down your front, through your chakras, as we said in the guided meditation portion of Chapter Six, and then up your spinal column to the top of the head. There, it rises to a height of twelve fingers above the crown of the head. This flow repeats itself over and over again.

When the energy rises—which you can encourage whether you are meditating, watching TV, shopping in the grocery store, wherever—when your energy rises, it discourages brain chemistry fluctuations such as anxiety, depression and panic. It really is difficult to have an anxiety attack if the energy is rising. Such attacks may indicate that you haven't fully opened the chakras and allowed for a complete flow, or anxiety attacks may show that the energy is being drained downward instead of rising. Maybe, too, you're allowing your energy to zip up the front instead of down the front and up the back. This happens when you let yourself move off center.

You also might be unwittingly permitting your energy to get stuck in your mind, and it's important to understand that rising energy is not energy rising into your mind. If your mind is allowed to waylay your energy, chemical imbalances are somewhat inevitable. Anxiety, depression, panic are forms of stuck energy, which will disappear as you learn to circulate the energy and allow it to rise. Remember, the energy is flowing down through the chakras and up your back through the crown of your head. The mind's role in this is what we discussed in Chapter Six: You are merging your mind into pure, infinite, unbounded Vital Force, which is a place where anxiety and depression are simply non-entities because it is a place of pure happiness.

The unfoldment of Vital Force happens as each of the chakras is turned. If you take your attention inside and hold it in a chakra long enough, you'll feel the subtle release we mentioned in the guided meditation. That subtle shift is described in some yoga texts as the opening and turning of the flower in you. When it turns upward, it does so to the next chakra and then to the next and so on, just as we practiced in the guided meditation. In other words, in this way, the Creative Energy in you is always rising up through the chakras. This discipline of opening the chakras and the rising up of the energy through them is called kundalini yoga.

In the guided meditation as well as in this chapter, I said your basic energy flows down through the chakras and up the spinal column. This may sound contradictory to what I've just said about the energy rising up through the chakras, but it isn't. The system of chakras is not one-inch deep in you. It is a channel which is core to you. On the simplest, physiological level, we know that if you have an injury to your chest, that injury will also effect the corresponding place in your back (to say nothing of your entire anatomy). On a higher and vaster plane, the same is true of chakras. When you open your heart chakra, you're not just opening something a few inches beneath the surface. You're opening something that, as you become more and more adept, can run so wide and so deep, if a camera could snap a picture of it, there would be no beginning and no end to the opening.

So as you practice meditation, do exactly as we said in Chapter Six—allow the energy to flow down the front and up the back—but understand that the energy in you, optimally, is always rising because it is circulating down and up, down and up, down and up, and after awhile, down and up become indistinguishable in up.

The interface between the physical and the spiritual in all of us is the cerebral-spinal fluid. Within that fluid, there are three different tides, and when we circulate the energy in meditation, we are actually tuning into these tides. There is the most basic or physical tide, which fluctuates ten times a minute, every minute, for as long as we exist. It fluctuates less if we're ill, but it fluctuates nonetheless for as long as we live. The absolute micro-second it ceases to fluctuate is the micro-second a person ceases to exist. Then there is a tide or dimension which is subtler; it is the energy of mind and perception. Finally, there is pure awareness within which all subjects and objects operate. This is Spirit.

At core, all three tides are one thing; our physical existence is inseparable from our mental existence which is inseparable from the breath of God, of Life, which is inseparable from our own breath, and so on. In other words, even the very fluid and breath in our bodies expresses that everything is One Thing. What could be more intimate and personal than the space between our own in-breath and out-breath; and yet isn't it the same space for everyone? Isn't it exactly *the* same space, not an identical space, but *the same* space—for everyone? What occupies the space when our breath has ceased in a given moment? Nothing but pure Awareness, nothing but Vital Force—nothing but One Thing.

In the traditional system of kundalini yoga, two chakras are emphasized: the one at the base of the spine and the chakra at the top of the head. The other chakras in the middle are important because if they're not open, then the two preeminent ones will not function. You may have noticed paintings of Hindu deities in which the deities sit on a lotus base. That base is the open chakra at the base of the spine; it is the energy base supporting the opening of the flowers of the chakras. The energy unfolds at the base in a petal-like fashion and then rises through the chakras to the top of the head. The lotus base is the opening; it is the expansion of your basic energy, and the full unfoldment of that energy is Self-realization.

In a state of Self-realization, the individual self has been reabsorbed into the Self, which is God. The energy has risen from the deadness of the physical body into a new Life, which is in no way limited. When each of the different chakras is in a perpetual state of openness and the energy has risen, Vital Force Itself becomes the sole focus of concern. In that state, we allow ourselves—our physical body and physical life—to become the instruments by which and through which Vital Force unfolds Its own creative expression—not *our* individual creative expression, but *Its* creative expression. In this state, we are beyond personhood; we don't think of ourselves as powerful or not powerful, strong or weak, enlightened or unenlightened. We have no personal agendas anymore. "What's going to happen to me?" is finished, "me" is finished, and we are living from the experience of Spirit and allowing our Life to unfold as It will.

From this perspective, death is not a concern but a cause for celebration because it represents a return of the iceberg to the ocean of Vital Force from which it was originally condensed. It represents a return of the body to its essence, to God. This understanding is real freedom. What will you fear when you realize that death is simply the return of your physical body to its natural home? What will you fear when you understand that all things are One Thing; that there is no "other" of which to be afraid?

From a state of Self-realization, the world and its apparent diversity, and any ups and downs intrinsic to it, are viewed as wondrous and rich because we see the underlying unity of it all. We see it as wondrous but unimportant because we understand that unity is everything. What thing will you want exactly when you know that all things are mere effects of that same Creative Energy you already have inside you?

In entering into a state of Self-realization, which has also traditionally been called divine contemplation, it takes some time for the residue of vibrations of our individual existence to be transformed into the subtle vibration intrinsic to Vital Force. During this period of transformation, every kind of desire and fear will rise up inside you. The reason is simple: As a higher, more powerful vibration is absorbed into your physical existence, the little self is not going to like the transformation very much because the little self loses the energy sustaining it when this happens. The ego is in effect sacrificed in this transformation. This is why rituals—whether Vedic, Hindu, or

Catholic—often focus on self-sacrifice. In meditation, we quiet our minds, center ourselves, and intensify our own vitality in order to surrender the self to the Self. The ritual of self-sacrifice, therefore, is about extending energy and merging the self into a finer field of experience.

So it's not surprising that the little self doesn't like this process and tries to lure our energy to a low level by scaring us about our practice, or waving every desire we ever flirted with under our noses, telling us that this time we can have it all if we just let go of this quest for Enlightenment. And that's when we have to choose. We can heed the call to growth, or we can get tangled up in the call of the little self. We can transcend the ocean of diversity, or we can drown in one inch of its water. It's up to us.

The recognition which arises from the experience of fully-risen kundalini or Self-realization is: There is no other. When we realize that the nature of Reality is One Thing, One Energy, diversity disappears and so, too, do striving, jealousy, anxiety, dis-ease, any notion of separateness. This is why, in Chapter Four, we talked about Self-dependence, not independence. The kind of separation from one another which independence implies is an illusion—it is one of those misunderstandings the mind has created in the face of diversity: me against her, us against them. The Reality is that at core, we are one.

Interdependence and interconnectedness are also not dependence. Each person has responsibility for his or her own growth, for the dissolution of the tensions and artificial boundaries which prevent an awareness of the boundlessness that is the Reality of our human essence.

Reality is one Creative Energy, Reality is Oneness, and when we understand this, we realize that leading a Life of unconditional love is not only possible, it's what's real. Whom will you hate when you understand it is all one Creative Energy? Whom will you forgive and for what, when you see that hurtful people are captivated by a world of diversity in which everything is completely difficult for them? Whom will you be jealous of; whom will you try to beat out of this position or that promotion? Whose heart will you steal and from whom?

Every person, whether you like him or not, whether you agree with her or not, every person is an expression of Vital Force, Divine Consciousness. Everything you do to someone, you are doing to yourself. It's not a constraint, it's a recognition; it is, in fact, true awareness. There is no such thing as any other person doing anything to you. Only if you're stuck in "me," do you think that way. To become entangled in your tensions, which manifest as your resistance to circumstances as well as your opinions about people, is to create a wall around yourself which suppresses the unfoldment of Creative Energy, which is Spirit.

So, really, when you understand that it is all one Spirit, whom will you hate? Whom will you forgive?

When we see that Life is fundamentally non-dualistic and therefore interconnected, we stand upon the principle of love.

The experience of the Oneness of the whole of Life automatically inclines us to see in each human being—compassionately inclines us to see—the same struggle